NEVEN MAGUIRE'S MIDWEEK MEALS

GILL BOOKS

Hume Avenue
Park West
Dublin 12
www.gillbooks.ie

Gill Books is an imprint of M.H. Gill and Co.

© Neven Maguire 2020

978 07171 89786

Compiled by Orla Broderick
Designed by www.grahamthew.com
Photography and props styling by Joanne Murphy
www.joanne-murphy.com
Assistants: James Butler, James Gavin, Clare Wilkinson
Food styling by Chloe Chan
Copy-edited by Kristin Jensen
Indexed by Eileen O'Neill
Printed and bound in Germany by Firmengruppe APPL

This book is typeset in DIN Regular.

DEDICATION

For my good friend Marty Whelan, who has been with me since day one on *Open House* to every Friday these days on Lyric FM. Over the years his cooking has improved, or so he says. He will devour this book! Marty, thank you for all the support, fun and laughs over the years.

ACKNOWLEDGEMENTS

It was a pleasure to work once again with the wonderful team at Gill Books. Nicki Howard sat me down and we came up with *Midweek Meals*, which I think is timely. So many people are taking up cooking at home and they will get plenty of ideas here. Once again the fabulous Orla Broderick worked on the recipes with me. I am delighted with the results. I love collaborating with Orla; her attention to detail is second to none.

Jo Murphy took the photos, which I love. She is so talented and put so much work into this book. Her assistants Clare Wilkinson, James Gavin and James Butler did a great job, and incidentally ate everything they were asked to!

Chloe Chan did the food styling. What a star. I am so impressed by the way she works and the results she gets.

James Whelan provided all the delicious meat. James has been a great friend and inspiration over the years. He is a master of his craft and I have long admired and respected the man and his work. Thank you also to O'Hanlon Fresh Herbs for supplying all the herbs we needed.

The Gill Books team of Catherine Gough, Teresa Daly, Ellen Monnelly and Paul Neilan oversaw editorial, publicity and sales, and, as always, were great to work with. Kristin Jensen is a brilliant copy-editor who makes sure she spots any errors in good time.

In the production of the book I get great help from the team at MacNean Restaurant and the cookery school. They are always there with ideas and are happy to test everything. Andrea Doherty makes sure everything happens. I would be lost without her. Restaurant Manager Bláthín McCabe, Assistant Manager Aidan Kelly and Head Chef Carmel McGirr are always on hand to help. As is my lovely wife, and lockdown camerawoman, Amelda. Yes, for all of those videos that people have been viewing, Amelda has been on the other side of the lens. A heartfelt thank you to all of our staff in MacNean.

Some of these recipes are ones that went down well at my cookery demonstrations, which could not happen without the help of our chef Claire Beasley, my brother Kenneth, who now has several demo units at work, and Eoin O'Flynn and John Rooney of Flogas. Thank you all.

Since my last book I have been enjoying working with Dunnes Stores on their Simply Better range and developing my cookware range, which is a dream come true for me. Thank you to Margaret Heffernan, Anne Heffernan and Sharon McMahon for inviting me to work with you. I love visiting with the great Irish producers that are now part of the Simply Better range. A big thank you to Diarmuid Murphy, Daragh Lawless and Derek Gallagher who head up the Simply Better team, and to Teresa Rafter, Michelle King and Nicola Bowman of the cookware team. A special thank you to the staff in Dunnes Stores in Donaghmede and Cornelscourt, who supplied all of the food for photography and could not have been more helpful.

Thanks also to my television crew of David Hare, Billy Keady, Ray de Brún, Andy Smith and

Helen Earley, and to Brian Walsh of RTÉ for his faith in us, and TVPR for their promotion of our programmes. Thank you also to the viewers who keep us there. Bord Bia give us great advice. Thank you Hylda Adams, Teresa Brophy and Tara McCarty.

Purcell Masterson in Kilkenny handle my media. Thank you to Sally Leadbetter, Anne Ryder and Emma McCreery, and to my agent John Masterson, who is always at the other end of the phone and has had the occasional good idea!

The Irish Farmers Journal are with me every single week. Thank you to Amii McKeever, Janine Kennedy, Ciara Leahy and Mairead Lavery. The Irish media have been supportive and kind over the years and I really appreciate it.

And, of course, there is Saturday radio on RTÉ. Brendan O'Connor is so knowledgeable about food. I have always enjoyed talking to him on radio and TV, but I never expected it to be on a Saturday morning. Driving to Dublin to chat with Marian Finucane was one of the most enjoyable parts of what I do. There would be the meticulous preparation by producer Anne Farrell, and then the pleasure of sitting in the studio with Marian with the time flying by. Judging by the reaction in the restaurant everyone listened to Marian. For her family, her colleagues in RTÉ and her audience to lose her so suddenly was a dreadful shock. I owe her so much and am happy that she and John were able to visit the restaurant on a few occasions. May she rest in peace.

It makes one realise the importance of family and, in that regard, I am blessed. Thank you to Amelda, Conor and Lucia for all of the happiness you bring.

CONTENTS

CUPBOARD'S BARE

SLOW AND LOW

INTRODUCTION

Even if you love to cook – as I do – getting dinner on the table for you and your family every evening can be quite an effort. You might have had a busy day at work or the kids need attention after school. In our house we have to factor in numerous after-school activities, which often require you to be in two places at once! People are dealing with different demands, so deciding what to make and then having the energy to cook it can certainly be a challenge.

One of the most important things that I have learned since becoming a dad is that a little preparation goes a long, long way. If you get the chance to plan out your meals at the weekend or on a day off, you will shop more efficiently and be able to give some thought to the balance of what you're eating. Otherwise, it's very easy to fall into the trap of having pasta five nights a week!

For most of us the weekend is an ideal time to plan. You might have the time to plan even a couple of midweek meals for those extremely busy days so that you only have to switch on the slow cooker before you leave in the morning. The slow cooker is a great invention. This will allow you to be more spontaneous on the other days, where you might use what's in your cupboard or do a quick supermarket sweep.

Whatever your approach, I'm hoping you will find that this book is jam-packed not only with delicious meal ideas, but also with thoroughly practical ones that you and your family will return to again and again.

No matter how busy life gets, I am a firm believer that it shouldn't be so busy that we can't enjoy our family time around the kitchen table and a home-cooked meal. Hopefully, this book will give you the inspiration, and the determination, to do just that.

ABOUT THE BOOK

This book is divided into four sections for every modern-life scenario:

1 ONE-PAN DINNERS

Time is tight or perhaps you just don't want a big pile of washing-up when you've finished cooking if you didn't even clean up before you left the house this morning. These one-pan wonders will help you get a delicious meal to the table – many of them in the time of a dishwasher cycle.

2 SUPERMARKET SWEEP

It's midweek and you are running out of ideas. If you can make a quick dash to the shop to pick up an ingredient or two, these recipes will give you a midweek boost.

3 CUPBOARD'S BARE

This is your emergency section! By taking the time once a month to stock your freezer and larder, you'll be surprised by what you can whip up when you think you've got nothing in.

4 SLOW AND LOW

These recipes work so well when you have a bit of time to soak some beans and prepare. Perhaps they will become your Monday favourites if you get into the habit of doing the prep on Sunday evening/ Monday morning. While the cooking time for these recipes is long, you'll have the prep done in a flash and will be free to go out and about while the dish is simmering away. Just switch on the slow cooker before you head off and come home to a delicious dinner – all ready! I used a Morphy Richards Sear and Stew 6.5 litre slow cooker for all the recipes.

THE SYMBOLS

You will see symbols at the top of each recipe, which will give you useful information at a glance. You'll see how long each recipe takes to prepare and cook, whether or not the dish freezes well (in which case, you could double up your efforts to have something for another day) and if the meal is packed with vegetable goodness.

 PREP TIME

 COOKING TIME

 LOTS OF VEGETABLES CRAMMED INTO THIS DISH

 THIS MEAL FREEZES PERFECTLY

MAKE YOUR LARDER AND FREEZER WORK FOR YOU

It's always handy to have some supplies in your larder and freezer as a back-up for those days when the cupboard is looking bare and you don't have time to get out to the shops. Tinned legumes can be turned into a hearty soup or stew, puff pastry in the freezer can be a godsend for a midweek pie and a good collection of spices can add zing to a dish that needs of a bit of oomph.

In addition to the long-life goods, some fresh veg and eggs will enable you to create many dishes – even when you think you have nothing in. A bit of larder/freezer management goes a long way, so here I have compiled my go-to stock items and the fresh produce I turn to when life is busy.

FRESH
- Lemons and limes
- Garlic
- Yoghurt
- Cheddar cheese/goat's cheese/Parmesan

FRIDGE
- Dijon mustard
- Caramelised onion marmalade
- Jars of roasted red peppers/artichokes/olives/capers/gherkins
- Chorizo/smoked bacon
- Prosciutto/Parma ham

FREEZER
- Frozen peas/petit pois
- Frozen sweetcorn
- Frozen spinach
- Frozen soya beans
- Frozen puff pastry
- Frozen sausages (or use fresh – easy to pick up)
- Frozen wraps and mini pizza bases
- Frozen broad beans

CUPBOARD
- Flour (plain and self-raising)
- Sugar
- Stock cubes (chicken and vegetable)
- Tins of coconut milk and coconut cream
- Pasta/polenta/orzo
- Dried vermicelli rice noodles
- Rice (risotto, basmati, long grain)
- Lentils/pearl barley
- Part-cooked bread (or even frozen sourdough)
- Tins of beans, lentils and tomatoes
- Tins of tuna
- Spices/harissa
- Rapeseed/cold pressed rapeseed oils
- Balsamic vinegar

CHAPTER 1 ONE-PAN DINNERS

25 MINS

 1 HR 20 MINS

 LOADS OF VEG

 FREEZER FRIENDLY

2 aubergines

2 tbsp rapeseed or olive oil, plus extra for brushing and drizzling

1 large onion, finely chopped

4 garlic cloves, crushed

1 × 400g (14oz) tin of Italian chopped tomatoes

1 tbsp tomato purée

1 × 400g (14oz) tin of chickpeas, drained and rinsed

6 ripe tomatoes, sliced

2 tsp chopped fresh flat-leaf parsley

sea salt and freshly ground black pepper

FOR THE TAHINI DRESSING

150g (5oz) natural yoghurt

50g (2oz) tahini (sesame seed paste)

juice of ½ lemon

50ml (2fl oz) water

good pinch of za'atar (see page 198 for more info)

Aubergine Moussaka with Tahini Dressing Serves 4–6

This vegetarian version of moussaka is much lighter than its traditional Greek counterpart, as the key flavour is an intense tomato sauce. Don't skip the tahini dressing – the flavour of the sesame seeds and cooling yoghurt is a fabulous contrast to the dish itself and rounds it off perfectly.

Chop one aubergine into bite-size cubes, place on a plate and cover with salt. Slice the other aubergine into rounds, place on a separate plate and also cover with salt. Set aside for 15 minutes to draw out all the bitter juices.

Rinse the aubergine slices and dry well with kitchen paper. Brush each one with oil and sauté in batches in an ovenproof frying pan that is approximately 25cm (10in) in diameter. Cook each batch for 8–10 minutes, turning once, until cooked through and golden brown. Transfer to a plate and set aside.

Heat 1 tablespoon of oil in the pan, then add the onion and sauté for 5 minutes, until softened. Rinse the cubed aubergines and pat dry with kitchen paper, then add to the pan with another tablespoon of oil. Cook for about 10 minutes, stirring occasionally, until the cubes have softened and turned golden.

Stir in the garlic and cook for a couple of minutes, until fragrant. Pour in the tinned tomatoes and tomato purée, season with salt and pepper and bring everything to a simmer. Cover and cook over the lowest heat for 15 minutes, stirring occasionally.

Meanwhile, preheat the oven to 200°C (400°F/gas mark 6).

Once the sauce is done, cover with the chickpeas, sliced ripe tomatoes and finally the sautéed aubergine slices, then drizzle with a little extra oil. Bake in the preheated oven for 20 minutes, until bubbling and golden on top.

To make the dressing, stir together the yoghurt, tahini and lemon juice with the water and season with za'atar to taste. Scatter the parsley over the moussaka and divide into portions, then arrange on warmed plates. Drizzle over the tahini dressing to serve.

15 MINS

 15 MINS

500g (1lb 2 oz) baby new potatoes, such as Jersey Royals or Charlotte

100g (4oz) watercress

200g (7oz) cooked baby beetroot, cut in half or quarters (vac-packed or from a jar)

200g (7oz) smoked trout, skin removed and flaked into large pieces

juice of ½ lemon

sea salt and freshly ground black pepper

FOR THE DRESSING

2 tbsp creamed horseradish

2 tbsp thick Greek yoghurt

2 tbsp cold pressed rapeseed oil

2 tsp caster sugar

1 tsp Dijon mustard

1 small bunch of fresh dill, chopped, with a few fronds reserved to garnish

Smoked Trout, New Potato and Baby Beet Salad Serves 4–6

This combination feels like an old friend, as I find myself coming back to it time and time again. Goatsbridge smoked trout is a fantastic product and worth seeking out, although it's now available in many of the major Irish supermarkets.

To make the dressing, put the horseradish in a screw-topped jar with the yoghurt, oil, sugar, mustard and dill. Shake vigorously to combine, then season to taste with salt and pepper.

Scrub the potatoes, then cut them into bite-size pieces, put in a pan of salted water and bring to a simmer. Cook for 10–12 minutes, until tender, then drain. While still warm, toss with 1 heaped tablespoon of the dressing, season with salt and pepper and allow to cool a little.

Tip the dressed potatoes onto a serving platter and scatter over the watercress. Arrange the beetroot over the top, followed by the smoked trout. Spoon the dressing over the salad and finish with the reserved dill sprigs, a squeeze of lemon, plenty of pepper and a sprinkling of salt.

20 MINS

 35 MINS

 LOADS OF VEG

 FREEZER FRIENDLY

2 tbsp rapeseed oil

1 onion, finely chopped

2 garlic cloves, crushed

1 sweet potato, peeled and cubed

2 tsp finely grated fresh root ginger

1 tbsp mild curry powder or paste
(I love the Dunnes Stores Simply
Better Mild Curry Seasoning)

1 × 400g (14oz) tin of Italian chopped
tomatoes

1 × 400ml (14fl oz) tin of coconut
milk

1 tbsp mango chutney

4 × 175g (6oz) boneless, skinless
chicken fillets, cut into 2.5cm (1in)
cubes

1 × 400g (14oz) tin of chickpeas,
drained and rinsed

200g (7oz) fresh or frozen spinach

juice of 1 lime

sea salt and freshly ground black
pepper

TO GARNISH

chopped fresh coriander or basil
leaves

TO SERVE

warmed flatbreads or pitta breads
(optional)

Quick Chicken Korma with Sweet Potatoes and Chickpeas
Serves 4–6

This quick and easy curry has everything you need in one bowl – it's nutritious, filling and packed full of goodness. It's also delicious made with monkfish instead of chicken. I like to serve it with warmed flatbreads or pitta breads for scooping it up, but you really don't need them.

Heat the oil in a large pan over a medium-high heat. Add the onion and garlic and fry for 4–6 minutes, until golden brown. Stir in the sweet potato and ginger and cook for 1 minute, stirring.

Add the curry powder or paste and a pinch of salt and cook for another minute, stirring. Add the tomatoes, coconut milk and mango chutney. Stir well to combine, then bring to a fast simmer for 3–5 minutes, stirring occasionally, until the sauce is so well reduced that it's almost sticking to the bottom of the pan.

Stir in the cubed chicken and slowly bring to the boil, then reduce the heat and simmer gently for 10–15 minutes, until the chicken is cooked through and completely tender. Add the rinsed chickpeas, spinach and lime juice and cook for a further 2–3 minutes. Season to taste.

Ladle into warmed bowls and scatter over the coriander or basil. Serve with warmed flatbreads or pitta breads, if liked.

20 MINS

 20 MINS

600ml (1 pint) chicken stock (from a cube is fine)

2 × 400ml (14fl oz) tins of coconut milk

juice of 1 lime

20g (¾oz) fresh galangal, peeled and sliced

3 dried kaffir lime leaves (I like the Thai Gold brand)

2 lemongrass stalks, trimmed and chopped

1–2 dried or fresh bird's eye chillies

2 tbsp Thai fish sauce (nam pla)

1 tbsp sweet chilli sauce

2 tsp tomato purée

400g (14oz) flat rice noodles

150g (5oz) shiitake mushrooms, thinly sliced

225g (8oz) boneless, skinless chicken fillets, diced

1 head of pak choi, thinly sliced

TO GARNISH

good handful of fresh coriander leaves

chilli oil

Thai Chicken Laksa with Pak Choi Serves 4–6

Laksa is a noodle soup found all over South-East Asia, where Thai fish sauce (nam pla) is used instead of salt and pepper. Adjust the amount of chilli and chilli oil to taste depending on how spicy you like your food.

Heat the chicken stock in a pan. Add the coconut milk, lime juice, galangal, lime leaves, lemongrass, chillies, fish sauce, sweet chilli sauce and tomato purée. Bring to the boil, stirring to combine, then reduce the heat and simmer for 5 minutes. Taste and adjust as you think necessary – you may think it needs a little extra of something.

Pass the soup through a fine mesh sieve into a clean pan. Add the noodles, mushrooms and chicken and bring back to the boil. Reduce the heat and simmer gently for about 5 minutes, until the chicken is tender and the noodles have softened. Stir in the pak choi and allow to simmer for another minute, until it still has a little crunch.

Ladle the laksa into deep warmed bowls and garnish with coriander and a drizzle of chilli oil to serve.

30 MINS

 1 HR

❄ FREEZER FRIENDLY

2 tbsp rapeseed oil

1 onion, finely chopped

2 small leeks, trimmed and thinly sliced

4 tbsp dry white wine

400ml (14fl oz) cream

675g (1½lb) mixed skinned and boned fish fillets, cut into bite-sized pieces (such as trout or salmon, hake and smoked cod or haddock)

225g (8oz) raw peeled tiger prawns, thawed if frozen

100g (4oz) frozen peas

2 tbsp chopped fresh flat-leaf parsley

pinch of cayenne pepper

1 × 320g (11¼oz) ready-rolled puff pastry sheet, thawed

1 egg, beaten with a pinch of salt

sea salt and freshly ground black pepper

TO SERVE

lightly dressed rocket

Fish Pot Pie
Serves 4-6

Everyone loves fish pie and to make this a one-pan dish I'm using an ovenproof frying pan, but if you don't have one, just make it in a frying pan and then transfer the mixture to a pie dish. Choose any selection of fish that you like depending on what is freshest and available. If you prefer, use a topping of mashed potatoes.

Preheat the oven to 200°C (400°F/gas mark 6).

Heat the oil in a 25cm (10in) ovenproof frying pan over a medium heat. Add the onion and leeks and cook for 4–5 minutes, until softened but not coloured. Pour in the wine and allow to bubble right down, then stir in the cream and cook for another 8–10 minutes, until well reduced and thickened.

Remove from the heat and stir in the fish, prawns, peas and parsley. Season to taste with salt and pepper and add the cayenne pepper. Stir gently to combine.

Unroll the pastry and use to cover the fish filling, trimming and cutting down as necessary, then pinch the edges to create a rim. Brush with the beaten egg wash and bake in the preheated oven for 30–35 minutes, until well-risen and golden brown.

Serve straight to the table with a separate bowl of rocket.

20 MINS

 15 MINS

 LOADS OF VEG

One-Pot Vegetable Pasta
Serves 4–6

600ml (1 pint) vegetable stock (from a cube is fine)

500g (1lb 2oz) fresh egg tortiglioni or rigatoni pasta

125g (4½oz) baby courgettes, trimmed and sliced on the diagonal

3 leeks, thinly sliced

200g (7oz) mixed baby peppers

2 garlic cloves, crushed

2–3 tbsp cold pressed rapeseed oil

½ tsp dried chilli flakes

300g (11oz) baby plum tomatoes, quartered

sea salt and freshly ground black pepper

TO GARNISH (OPTIONAL)

chopped fresh flat-leaf parsley

toasted pine nuts

freshly grated Parmesan cheese

This has to be the ultimate easy weeknight dinner, as you just throw everything into a pan and you're done. It's clever, too, as the starch from the pasta creates a creamy sauce that we've come to love in our house.

Put all the ingredients except the tomatoes in a large pan and season with salt. Bring to the boil over a medium heat, then cover, reduce the heat and simmer for 4–6 minutes. Give everything a good stir after a couple of minutes to make sure nothing is sticking to the bottom of the pan.

Fold in the tomatoes and season with pepper, then divide into wide-rimmed bowls and scatter over the parsley, pine nuts and Parmesan (if using).

15 MINS

 15 MINS

Warm Goat's Cheese Salad with Peppers and Candied Pecans
Serves 4–6

4–6 long slices of baguette (preferably sourdough)

1 × 290g (10¼oz) jar of roasted peppers in oil

325g (11½oz) firm goat's cheese, sliced (see the intro)

100g (4oz) baby spinach leaves (use nice small leaves)

50g (2oz) frisée salad leaves

4 tbsp sliced black olives

about 1 tsp balsamic vinegar

sea salt and freshly ground black pepper

FOR THE CANDIED PECANS

100g (4oz) pecan nuts

25g (1oz) butter, diced

2 tbsp light muscovado sugar

This is an impressive salad that would be nice enough to serve at a relaxed dinner party or a special midweek dinner with your family. It takes very little time to get on the table. I always use the classic French chevre blanc that comes in a log with a rind so that it can be cut into handy rounds.

Preheat the oven to 200°C (400°F/gas mark 6).

Spread the pecan nuts on a baking sheet and cook in the preheated oven for 5–6 minutes, until toasted. Remove from the oven and using a spoon, quickly toss in the butter and sugar until the sugar has completely dissolved. Turn out onto a plate, season with salt and pepper and leave to cool and harden.

Arrange the slices of baguette on a baking sheet and bake in the oven for 3–4 minutes, until lightly toasted.

Meanwhile, drain the oil from the peppers and reserve, then cut the peppers into thin strips. Remove the baguettes from the oven and drizzle lightly with a little of the reserved oil, then arrange the goat's cheese on top and bake for another 3–4 minutes, until just beginning to bubble and turn golden.

Meanwhile, place the baby spinach and frisée on plates or in shallow bowls, then scatter over the peppers and olives. Drizzle over a little of the reserved pepper oil and enough balsamic vinegar to lightly coat the leaves. Season with salt and pepper, then scatter over the candied pecan nuts. Arrange the goat's cheese toasts on top to serve.

20 MINS

 25 MINS

 LOADS OF VEG

 FREEZER FRIENDLY

3 tbsp rapeseed oil

1 onion, grated

6 whole cardamom pods, lightly crushed to split them open

1 tsp chilli powder

½ tsp ground turmeric

1 cinnamon stick

3 garlic cloves, finely grated

1 × 2.5cm (1in) piece of fresh root ginger, finely grated

1 small bunch of fresh coriander

250ml (9fl oz) coconut cream

120ml (4fl oz) vegetable stock (from a cube is fine)

300g (11oz) organic Irish salmon, skinned, boned and diced

200g (7oz) hake, skinned, boned and diced

225g (8oz) mangetout, halved

225g (8oz) sugar snap peas, halved

225g (8oz) fine green beans, trimmed and halved

pinch of salt

TO GARNISH

lime wedges

TO SERVE

mini Peshwari naan breads

South Indian Fish Curry with Green Vegetables
Serves 4–6

This curry originates from the tropical south coast of India. Keralan-style fish curry is traditionally served with jasmine rice and green beans, but I've bulked it up with extra vegetables that I've gently poached in the broth, then served it with some delicious mini Peshwari naan breads, which are available in all major supermarkets.

Heat a heavy-based pan with 2 tablespoons of the oil over a medium heat. Add the onion and cook for 2–3 minutes, until softened but not coloured, then add the cardamom pods, chilli powder and turmeric. Cook for 1–2 minutes, stirring constantly, until fragrant.

Stir the remaining oil into the pan along with the cinnamon stick, garlic and ginger. Cook for another 1–2 minutes, until the garlic and ginger have softened and are cooked through.

Reserve a few coriander sprigs for garnish, then blend the remainder with the coconut cream in a mini food processor (don't worry if it looks a bit split). Stir into the pan with the stock and bring to the boil, then reduce the heat and simmer gently for 1–2 minutes.

Stir in the fish and vegetables and season with salt. Continue to simmer for 1–2 minutes, stirring constantly, until the fish and vegetables are all cooked through and tender.

Garnish the curry with the reserved coriander sprigs and lime wedges and serve at once with the mini Peshwari naan breads.

15 MINS

 55 MINS

 FREEZER FRIENDLY

1 large onion, finely chopped

2 carrots, chopped

2 celery sticks, chopped

2 garlic cloves, finely chopped

3 bay leaves

1 tsp chopped fresh thyme, plus extra to garnish

1.7 litres (3 pints) water

2 chicken stock cubes

4 boneless, skinless chicken fillets

175g (6oz) orzo (see the intro)

2 tbsp roughly chopped fresh flat-leaf parsley

sea salt and freshly ground black pepper

TO SERVE

sourdough baguette and butter

Poached Chicken and Orzo Soup Serves 4-6

Orzo is a rice-shaped pasta that is brilliant to use in soups, salads and all kinds of pasta dishes. It looks like a type of grain and is categorised as pastina in Italy, which means 'little pasta'. It's actually a very popular ingredient all over Europe, particularly in Greece, where it's called kritharaki.

To make the stock, place the onion, carrots, celery, garlic, bay leaves and thyme in a large pan with the water. Bring to the boil, then crumble in the stock cubes and simmer for 20 minutes, until the vegetables have released their flavour.

Reduce the heat to low, then add the chicken fillets and poach for 12–15 minutes, until tender. Transfer to a plate and leave to cool for 5 minutes.

Meanwhile, stir the orzo into the pan and simmer for 8–10 minutes, until tender.

When the chicken has rested for 5 minutes, shred the meat using two forks and return to the soup while the orzo is finishing cooking. Season to taste with salt and pepper.

Ladle the chicken and orzo soup into bowls (discarding the bay leaves) and scatter the extra thyme and the parsley on top. Serve with chunks of sourdough baguette spread with butter.

15 MINS

 20 MINS

Spaghetti with Prawns, Salmon and Mussels Serves 4-6

900g (2lb) live mussels, well cleaned (see the intro)

2 tbsp dry white wine

2 garlic cloves, crushed

1 fresh red chilli, deseeded and finely chopped

600ml (1 pint) cream

500g (1lb 2oz) fresh egg spaghetti

200g (7oz) raw peeled tiger prawns

175g (6oz) fresh salmon fillets, skinned and cut into small cubes

1 tbsp shredded fresh basil

1 tbsp chopped fresh flat-leaf parsley

sea salt and freshly ground black pepper

TO GARNISH

lemon wedges

TO SERVE

crusty French baguette

This is a simple white wine cream sauce for any pasta dish. You could also use a mixture of seafood if you want something on the table super quick, or if you really want to push the boat out, lobster. Wash the mussels in plenty of cold water and scrub the shells with a stiff brush, then use a knife to scrape off any barnacles that are sticking to them. Pull out the tough, fibrous beards protruding from the tightly closed shells. Discard any mussels that do not close when lightly tapped on the work surface.

Place the mussels in a pan with a lid and pour over the wine. Cover tightly and cook over a high heat for a few minutes, shaking the pan occasionally until all the mussels have opened – discard any that do not. Strain through a sieve, reserving the cooking liquor, and leaving behind any grit. Reserve some mussels to garnish and remove the rest from their shells.

Pour the reserved mussel liquor back into the pan and add the garlic, chilli and cream. Bring to the boil, then reduce the heat, stir in the spaghetti and simmer for 2 minutes. Stir in the prawns and salmon and simmer gently for another 2 minutes.

Fold in the mussels, basil and parsley until well combined, then season with salt and pepper.

To serve, divide the spaghetti with the prawns, salmon and mussels between warmed bowls. Garnish with the reserved mussels and lemon wedges and serve with a separate bowl of crusty French baguette.

15 MINS

 1 HR

 LOADS OF VEG

Roast Chicken Red Curry with Sweet Potatoes and Kale
Serves 4–6

1 × 400ml (14fl oz) tin of coconut milk

4 tbsp Thai red curry paste

2 tbsp Thai fish sauce (nam pla)

good pinch of caster sugar

4 dried kaffir lime leaves (I like the Thai Gold brand)

1 lemongrass stalk

8 large chicken thighs, bone in and skin on, trimmed (preferably free-range or organic)

675g (1½lb) sweet potatoes, cut into wedges

450g (1lb) kale, tough stalks removed and leaves shredded

pinch of salt

This has all the flavour of a curry, but in a one-pan supper. The chicken thighs become succulent and tender braised in the spicy broth – you'll find yourself transported to Thailand!

Preheat the oven to 180°C (350°F/gas mark 4).

Place the coconut milk, curry paste, fish sauce, sugar, lime leaves and lemongrass stalk in a deep-sided baking tin and mix well to combine. Rub the chicken thighs with salt and place them in the baking tin, skin side up, tucking the sweet potatoes around them. Cover with tin foil and roast in the preheated oven for 30 minutes.

Increase the oven temperature to 200°C (400°F/gas mark 6), remove the foil and roast for another 15 minutes, until the chicken is meltingly tender and the skin is crispy.

Using a tongs, transfer the chicken to a plate, cover loosely with foil and leave to rest. Skim any excess fat from the sauce and fold in the kale, then return to the oven for another 6–8 minutes, until the kale has wilted and the sweet potatoes are cooked through and tender. Arrange on plates to serve.

20 MINS

 40 MINS

 LOADS OF VEG

 FREEZER FRIENDLY

Harissa Lamb and Butternut Squash Curry
Serves 4–6

1 tbsp rapeseed oil

500g (1lb 2oz) boneless lamb, cut into bite-sized pieces

1 large onion, finely chopped

2 garlic cloves, finely chopped

1 × 2.5cm (1in) piece of fresh root ginger, peeled and grated

1 × 2.5cm (1in) piece of fresh turmeric (optional)

4–6 tbsp harissa paste

250ml (9fl oz) Greek yoghurt

1 × 400g (14oz) tin of Italian chopped tomatoes

1 butternut squash, peeled, seeds removed and cut into cubes

2 large handfuls of baby spinach

TO GARNISH

toasted flaked almonds

TO SERVE

soft white wraps

shop-bought tzatziki

This clever curry is quick and tasty and uses harissa paste for its kick, but you could also use a tablespoon of your favourite curry powder or paste instead. If you prefer a smooth sauce, then simply blend with a hand-held blender before adding the butternut squash, which could be replaced by regular or sweet potatoes.

Heat the oil in a large pan over a medium heat. Add the lamb and sauté until well browned all over, then transfer to a plate. Add the onion to the pan and cook for 2–3 minutes, then add the garlic, ginger and turmeric (if using) and cook for another minute or so.

Stir in the harissa paste to taste, then add the yoghurt one large spoonful at a time, stirring continuously. Stir in the tomatoes and butternut squash. Fold in the browned lamb, then cover with a lid and cook gently for 25–30 minutes, until the lamb and butternut squash are tender.

Stir in the spinach and allow to wilt and warm through. Garnish with toasted flaked almonds and serve with soft white wraps and tzatziki.

25 MINS

 40 MINS

 LOADS OF VEG

 FREEZER FRIENDLY (CHICKEN)

Coriander and Honey-Glazed Chicken with Shopska Salad
Serves 4–6

5 tbsp clear honey

2 tbsp freshly grated root ginger

4 tsp coriander seeds, coarsely ground

4 tsp fennel seeds

4 chicken thighs

4 chicken drumsticks

sea salt and freshly ground black pepper

FOR THE SHOPSKA SALAD

3 large ripe tomatoes, cut into cubes

1 cucumber, cut into cubes

1 green pepper, cut into cubes

1 bunch of spring onions, trimmed and roughly chopped

3 tbsp rapeseed oil

3 tbsp white wine vinegar

150g (5oz) feta cheese

10 black olives

1 small bunch of fresh flat-leaf parsley, leaves stripped and finely chopped

This salad originates in Bulgaria and is named after the Shoppi, or natives of Sofia. It's perfect in the summertime, when the tomatoes are at their most flavoursome. Here it accompanies tasty chicken pieces, which are good value in the supermarket.

Preheat the oven to 200°C (400°F/gas mark 6).

To make the glaze for the chicken, mix together the honey, ginger, coriander and fennel in a small bowl.

Heat a heavy-based frying pan until very hot. Season the chicken and place skin side down in the heated frying pan. Cook for 2–3 minutes, until browned, then turn over and brush with the glaze. Transfer to a baking tray and cook in the preheated oven for a further 30–35 minutes, until the chicken is cooked through and tender.

Meanwhile, make the Shopska salad. Mix together the tomatoes, cucumber, green pepper and spring onions in a large bowl. Drizzle with the oil and vinegar, tossing to combine, then divide between plates. Crumble over the feta cheese, then scatter over the olives and parsley. Arrange the chicken alongside to serve.

20 MINS

 15 MINS

Thai-Style Chicken Noodles with Green Beans
Serves 4-6

4 tbsp soy sauce

2 tbsp Thai fish sauce (nam pla)

2 tbsp clear honey

2 tsp light muscovado sugar

3 tbsp rapeseed oil

2 large shallots, thinly sliced

2 garlic cloves, thinly sliced

1 fresh long red chilli, deseeded and thinly sliced into rings

4 boneless, skinless chicken fillets, cut into bite-sized pieces

200g (7oz) fine green beans, trimmed and cut in half

juice of 1 lime

2 × 150g (5oz) packets of straight-to-wok noodles

50g (2oz) fresh bean sprouts, trimmed

TO GARNISH

fresh coriander leaves

Straight-to-wok noodles are a brilliant shortcut if you're in a hurry and want to save on washing up. They only need to be heated through, but don't be tempted to overcook them or they will break up into small pieces.

Place the soy sauce in a small bowl and stir in the fish sauce, honey and sugar. Set aside until needed.

Heat a wok until smoking hot. Add the oil and swirl it up the sides, then tip in the shallots, garlic and chilli. Stir-fry for 1–2 minutes, until sizzling.

Tip the chicken into the wok and continue to stir-fry for 2–3 minutes, until sealed. Drizzle over the soy sauce mixture and cook for another 1–2 minutes, until the chicken is nicely glazed.

Add the green beans to the chicken mixture, then sprinkle over the lime juice and stir-fry for 2–3 minutes, until the green beans are cooked through but still have a little bite. Fold in the noodles and allow to just warm through. Add the bean sprouts and cook for 30 seconds or so to keep them crisp.

Arrange in warmed bowls and scatter over the coriander leaves to serve.

20 MINS

 20 MINS

 LOADS OF VEG

Chargrilled Lamb, Courgette and Halloumi Salad
Serves 4-6

3 tbsp rapeseed oil

1 tbsp honey

3 garlic cloves, crushed

1 heaped tsp chopped fresh oregano, rosemary or thyme (or use a mixture), plus extra to garnish

4–6 × 150g (5oz) lamb leg steaks

2 green courgettes, thinly sliced lengthways into ribbons

1 yellow courgette, thinly sliced lengthways into ribbons

250g (9oz) halloumi, cut into 12 slices

1 lemon, cut into wedges

100g (4oz) baby plum tomatoes, halved

sea salt and freshly ground black pepper

TO SERVE

shop-bought tzatziki

baby spinach salad

wholemeal wraps

This dish would also be delicious all cooked on the barbecue on a nice sunny evening. Even the lemon benefits from being chargrilled, turning its juice into a delicious caramelised dressing.

Preheat a griddle pan over a medium-high heat.

Mix together the oil, honey, garlic and herbs in a small bowl and season with salt and pepper. Brush all over the lamb, courgettes and halloumi.

Add the lamb to the griddle pan and cook for 3 minutes on each side, until medium-rare, or continue until cooked to your liking. Transfer to a plate to rest, cover loosely with foil and keep warm.

Add the courgettes to the pan and sear for 2–3 minutes on each side, until cooked through and tender. Transfer to a plate and set aside until needed.

Add the halloumi and lemon wedges to the griddle pan. Cook the halloumi for 30 seconds on each side and the lemon until nicely chargrilled.

Arrange the courgette salad on plates with the chargrilled lamb and halloumi. Scatter over the baby plum tomatoes and add a dollop of tzatziki to each plate, then scatter over the herbs to garnish and add the lemon wedges. Serve with baby spinach salad and wholemeal wraps.

10 MINS

 20 MINS

 LOADS OF VEG

Chilli Beef and Vegetable Rice Noodles with Peanuts
Serves 4-6

350g (12oz) dried vermicelli rice noodles

500g (1lb 2oz) thin beef frying steaks

1 tbsp rapeseed oil, plus a little extra for brushing

1 bunch of spring onions, trimmed and thinly sliced on the diagonal

1 large red pepper, very thinly sliced

4 pak choi, sliced

200g (7oz) fresh bean sprouts

75g (3oz) dry-roasted peanuts, chopped

2 tbsp dark soy sauce

2 tbsp sweet chilli sauce, plus extra to serve

sea salt and freshly ground black pepper

TO GARNISH

fresh coriander leaves

I love noodles for one-pot dishes, as they only need to be soaked and don't take up an extra pan! Even if the instructions on the packet recommend cooking them, they will always soften as described below. They are perfect for soaking up spicy flavours and if you keep them in a bowl of water until you're ready to use them, they will never stick.

Put the noodles in a large flat dish and cover with boiling water. Set aside for 2 minutes to soften, then drain and rinse under cold running water. Leave in cold water to prevent them from sticking.

Season the steaks with salt and pepper and brush with oil. Heat a large wok or non-stick frying pan over a high heat, then add the steaks and sear for 1–2 minutes, so they are still pink in the middle. Transfer to a plate and leave to rest for 5 minutes before slicing. Keep warm by covering loosely with foil.

Drain the noodles. Add the oil to the wok, then add the spring onions, red pepper and pak choi and stir-fry for 2–3 minutes, until tender. Toss in the noodles with the bean sprouts and most of the peanuts. Drizzle with the soy and sweet chilli sauce and stir-fry for 1 minute to heat through. Season to taste with a light sprinkling of salt and plenty of black pepper.

Divide the noodles between bowls and arrange the slices of beef on top. Drizzle over a little extra sweet chilli sauce and scatter the remaining peanuts and the fresh coriander leaves on top to serve.

25 MINS

 1 HR 15 MINS

 LOADS OF VEG

 FREEZER FRIENDLY

6 ears of corn on the cob (husks still intact)

2 tbsp rapeseed oil

1 large onion, finely chopped

3 celery sticks, finely chopped

1 large potato, peeled and finely chopped (about 300g (11oz))

2 garlic cloves, finely chopped

2 litres (3½ pints) chicken or vegetable stock (from a cube is fine)

1 large handful of fresh basil leaves

150ml (¼ pint) cream

sea salt and freshly ground black pepper

TO GARNISH

piri piri marinade or chilli oil (optional)

Roasted Corn and Basil Chowder Serves 4–6

You could speed this recipe up and just use 500g (1lb 2oz) of frozen sweetcorn, but you won't get the depth of flavour and smokiness of this version. Corn on the cob is really good value when in season and it makes the most fantastic soup. This is fresh and vibrant and light enough for summer.

Preheat the oven to 180°C (350°F/gas mark 4).

Place the cobs of corn in their husks on a baking sheet and roast in the preheated oven for about 45 minutes. Remove from the oven and set aside until cool enough to handle. Cut the kernels of corn off the cobs into a bowl, then discard the cobs, husks and silk.

Meanwhile, heat the oil in a large pan over a medium heat. Add the onion and celery and sauté for 8–10 minutes, until soft but not coloured. Stir in the potatoes and garlic, then pour in the stock. Bring to the boil, then reduce the heat and simmer for 10–15 minutes, until the potatoes are very soft and beginning to break up in the soup.

Add the corn kernels, reserving a couple of handfuls to garnish, and simmer for about 5 minutes, until heated through. Season with salt and pepper and add most of the basil and all the cream, then using a hand-held blender, purée the soup until smooth.

Ladle the roasted corn and basil chowder into bowls and top with the reserved sweetcorn kernels and reserved basil. If you like a bit of heat, drizzle each one with a little piri piri marinade or chilli oil.

10 MINS

 25 MINS

Plaice Florentine with Butter Beans and Mushrooms
Serves 4-6

2 tbsp softened butter

250g (9oz) open-cup chestnut mushrooms, sliced

2 garlic cloves, finely chopped

1 × 400g (14oz) tin of butter beans, drained and rinsed

150g (5oz) baby spinach

4 large skinless plaice fillets, each fillet cut in half

2 tsp rapeseed oil

juice of ½ lemon

4 tbsp freshly grated Parmesan cheese

sea salt and freshly ground black pepper

Butter beans are large, creamy-coloured beans that have a soft, floury texture that makes them extremely versatile. They actually go surprisingly well with the plaice in this dish and save you having to cook some potatoes.

Melt half the butter in a large non-stick frying pan over a medium heat. When sizzling, add the mushrooms and season generously with salt and pepper, then cook for 5–6 minutes, until tender. Tip out onto a plate and set aside.

Add the remaining butter to the frying pan, then add the garlic and sauté for 30–60 seconds, until sizzling. Toss in the butter beans and continue to sauté for 1–2 minutes. Stir in the spinach until just wilted and season to taste with salt and pepper.

Preheat the grill to its highest setting.

Arrange the plaice fillets on top of the butter bean and spinach mixture in a single layer, then drizzle with the oil and lemon juice and season to taste with salt and pepper. Grill for 4 minutes, keeping the handle of the frying pan well away from the heat.

Scatter the mushrooms over the fish and sprinkle with the Parmesan. Return to the grill for another 3–4 minutes, until the Parmesan is golden and bubbling. Serve immediately straight to the table.

15 MINS

 20 MINS

Chilli Salt Salmon with Chestnut Mushrooms
Serves 4–6

2 garlic cloves, finely grated

1 small piece of fresh root ginger, peeled and finely grated

4 tbsp kecap manis (sweet soy sauce)

120ml (4fl oz) water

1 tbsp sea salt flakes

1 tbsp dried chilli flakes

4 × 175g (6oz) boneless salmon fillets, skinned

1 tbsp rapeseed oil

1 red onion, thinly sliced

200g (7oz) baby chestnut mushrooms, thinly sliced

250g (9oz) dried vermicelli rice noodles

TO GARNISH

fresh coriander leaves

Kecap manis is a sweetened aromatic Malay/Indonesian sauce with a consistency resembling maple syrup. It's made from fermented soy sweetened with palm sugar molasses. It's brilliant for adding a mild sweet and umami flavour to lots of dishes and is also great as a dipping sauce on its own.

Place the garlic, ginger and kecap manis in a bowl and stir in the water. Set aside until needed.

Mix together the sea salt and chilli flakes on a plate, then press in both sides of the salmon to coat. Using a sharp knife, cut the salmon into 1cm (½in) pieces.

Heat the oil in a large wok or non-stick frying pan over a high heat. Add the salmon in batches and cook for 1 minute on each side. Transfer to a plate and set aside.

Add the red onion and mushrooms to the wok and stir-fry for 2 minutes. Pour over the reserved sauce and cook for another 3–4 minutes, until the veg are tender.

Meanwhile, pour boiling water over the noodles and leave for 2 minutes or according to the packet instructions.

Drain the noodles and divide between plates, then arrange the salmon on top. Spoon over the sauce and scatter over the coriander to serve.

25 MINS

 30 MINS

 LOADS OF VEG

Jewelled Couscous Salad with Sweet Onions and Cherry Tomatoes Serves 4–6

500g (1lb 2oz) couscous

6 tbsp cold pressed rapeseed oil

750ml (1¼ pints) boiling water

2 large onions, cut into rings 2mm (¼in) thick (about 1kg (2¼lb) in total)

1 tsp honey

½ tsp mild curry powder (I love the Dunnes Stores Simply Better Mild Curry Seasoning) or ras el hanout

75g (3oz) mix of golden raisins and dried cranberries (available together in packets)

1 × 400g (14oz) tin of chickpeas, drained and rinsed

75g (3oz) toasted blanched almonds or pistachio nuts, roughly chopped

20g (¾oz) fresh flat-leaf parsley, leaves stripped and roughly chopped

20g (¾oz) fresh dill or fennel fronds, fronds stripped and roughly chopped

20g (¾oz) fresh basil, leaves stripped and shredded

1 garlic clove, crushed

2 tbsp lemon juice

1 tsp cumin seeds, toasted and lightly crushed

2 × 250g (9oz) packets of mixed cherry tomatoes (different colours), halved

sea salt and freshly ground black pepper

This is a fantastic salad that can be made well in advance and served at room temperature. For a change you could use pearl couscous, which is now becoming more readily available, and just follow the instructions on the packet.

Put the couscous in a large bowl and season with ½ teaspoon of salt. Drizzle over 2 tablespoons of the oil, then pour over the boiling water. Cover with cling film and leave to soak for 10 minutes.

Meanwhile, heat a large frying pan over a medium to high heat. Add 2 tablespoons of the oil, then tip in the onions and sprinkle over ¼ teaspoon each of salt and pepper along with the honey and the mild curry powder or ras el hanout. Sauté for 20–25 minutes, until the onions are well softened and catching around the edges. Remove from the heat and stir in the golden raisins and cranberries.

Remove the cling film from the couscous and fluff up with a fork, then stir in the onion and dried fruit mixture along with the chickpeas, almonds or pistachio nuts, herbs, garlic, lemon juice, cumin and the remaining 2 tablespoons of oil. Season to taste and tip out onto a large serving platter. Scatter the tomatoes over the couscous mixture and gently fold them in to serve.

20 MINS

 1 HR

 LOADS OF VEG

 FREEZER FRIENDLY

450g (1lb) sweet potatoes, peeled and cut into cubes

2 tbsp rapeseed oil

1 onion, finely chopped

1 leek, finely chopped

1 lemongrass stalk, trimmed and halved

½ fresh red chilli, deseeded and finely chopped

1 tsp freshly grated root ginger

1.2 litres (2 pints) chicken or vegetable stock (from a cube is fine)

1 tbsp tomato purée

250ml (9fl oz) coconut milk

1 × 400g (14oz) tin of chickpeas, drained and rinsed

sea salt and freshly ground black pepper

TO GARNISH

toasted coconut flakes

fresh basil leaves

TO SERVE

sourdough baguette (optional)

Sweet Potato Soup with Chickpeas and Coconut
Serves 4–6

Despite their name, sweet potatoes are a root vegetable that, unlike regular potatoes, count as one of your seven a day. I love them in soup for the lovely soft velvety texture they give, but I tend to use them a lot as they are a great source of fibre and vitamins B and C. They are also high in an antioxidant known as beta-carotene, which converts to vitamin A once eaten.

Preheat the oven to 200°C (400°F/gas mark 6).

Place the sweet potatoes in a baking tin, drizzle over 1 tablespoon of the oil and roast in the preheated oven for 20–25 minutes, until tender. Set aside.

Heat the remaining tablespoon of oil in a pan. Add the onion, leek, lemongrass, chilli and ginger and sweat for 4 minutes, stirring occasionally. Add the roasted sweet potatoes with the stock and tomato purée, then bring to the boil, stirring. Reduce the heat and simmer for 10 minutes, until the liquid has slightly reduced and all the vegetables are completely tender.

Pour the coconut milk into the pan, add the chickpeas and cook for another 5 minutes, stirring constantly. Season to taste and remove the pieces of lemongrass.

Ladle the soup into warmed bowls, then scatter over the toasted coconut flakes and basil leaves as a garnish. Serve immediately with sourdough baguette if liked.

20 MINS

 30 MINS

 LOADS OF VEG

 FREEZER FRIENDLY

Vegetable and Vermicelli Curry with Lime and Coconut
Serves 4-6

2 × 20g (¾oz) packets of fresh coriander, roughly chopped

2 large garlic cloves, roughly chopped

1 × 5cm (2in) piece of fresh root ginger, peeled and roughly chopped

2 fresh long green chillies, deseeded and roughly chopped

1 bunch of spring onions, trimmed and roughly chopped

finely grated rind and juice of 1 lime

1 tsp caster sugar

50g (2oz) toasted coconut flakes

6 tbsp rapeseed oil

2 aubergines, trimmed and cubed

175g (6oz) dried vermicelli rice noodles

600ml (1 pint) vegetable stock (from a cube is fine)

1 × 400ml (14fl oz) tin of coconut milk

2 × 200g (7oz) packets of tenderstem broccoli, halved

200g (7oz) sugar snap peas, halved lengthways

This simple curry makes its own wonderfully fragrant green paste, which is so much fresher and more vibrant than anything you will ever buy in a jar. I've held some back and mixed it with some shredded coconut for garnishing, which gives the dish an extra dimension.

Place the coriander, garlic, ginger, chillies, spring onions, lime rind and sugar in a small food processor and blitz to a coarse paste. Place 1 heaped tablespoon in a bowl and mix in the toasted coconut flakes. Set aside until needed as garnish at the end.

Add 2 tablespoons of the oil to the food processor and blend until the spice paste is smooth. Heat the remaining 4 tablespoons of oil in a large wok or non-stick frying pan over a high heat. Add the paste and cook for 1 minute, until fragrant. Add the aubergines, stirring to combine, then reduce the heat to low. Cook for 10 minutes, until lightly golden and nearly tender.

Meanwhile, soak the rice noodles in a bowl of just-boiled water for 2 minutes or according to the packet instructions. Drain and rinse under cold running water to prevent them from cooking further. Put them back into a bowl of water to make sure they don't stick.

Add the stock and coconut milk to the wok and increase the heat to high to bring to a simmer. Tip in the tenderstem broccoli and sugar snap peas and cook for 2–3 minutes, until all the vegetables are just tender. Stir in the lime juice to taste.

Drain the noodles and divide between bowls, then ladle in the vegetable mixture. Sprinkle over the reserved coconut mixture to serve.

15 MINS

 15 MINS

Piquant Crab Spaghetti with Asparagus and Baby Courgettes
Serves 4-6

350g (12oz) good-quality spaghetti (such as Dunnes Stores Simply Better Bronze Die DOP Spaghetti)

3 tbsp rapeseed oil

1–2 fresh small red chillies, deseeded and very finely chopped

1 garlic clove, finely chopped

1 × 125g (4½oz) packet of baby courgettes, pared into ribbons

1 × 100g (4oz) packet of asparagus spears, pared into ribbons

200g (7oz) crab meat (fresh or frozen – see the intro)

finely pared rind and juice of 1 lemon

3 tbsp roughly chopped fresh flat-leaf parsley

sea salt and freshly ground black pepper

You could use frozen or pasteurised crab meat, but for a dish as simple as this, fresh is best if you can get hold of it. Ask your local fishmonger – you might be surprised that they actually do stock small quantities of it for favoured customers! I love this with a salad of fine herbs on top and a glass of chilled Sancerre on the side.

Cook the spaghetti in a large pan of boiling salted water until al dente (just tender to the bite), then drain.

Quickly return the pan to the heat. Add the oil, chilli to taste and the garlic and stir-fry for 1 minute, then toss in the courgettes and asparagus and stir-fry for another minute, until just softened.

Return the drained spaghetti to the pan with the crab meat and lemon juice to taste, then season with salt and pepper. Reduce the heat and continue to warm through for 1–2 minutes. Finally, fold in the parsley and divide between warmed bowls, then scatter over the lemon rind to serve.

20 MINS

 50 MINS

 LOADS OF VEG

 FREEZER FRIENDLY

4 tbsp rapeseed oil

2 garlic cloves, crushed

1 × 4cm (1½in) piece of fresh root ginger, peeled and grated

2 onions, chopped

600ml (1 pint) water

8 ripe tomatoes, chopped, or 1 × 400g (14oz) tin of Italian chopped tomatoes

2 tsp ground cumin

2 tsp garam masala

1 tsp paprika

1 tsp ground turmeric

½ tsp cayenne pepper

1 large cauliflower, cut into florets (about 500g (1lb 2oz) in total)

2 × 400g (14oz) tins of chickpeas, drained and rinsed

2 tbsp chopped fresh coriander

sea salt and freshly ground black pepper

TO SERVE

coriander and garlic naan bread

natural yoghurt

mango chutney

Spicy Cauliflower and Chickpea Curry
Serves 4-6

The curry sauce can be made well in advance – it will keep in the fridge for up to three days and it also freezes very well. You could always add diced chicken or tender lamb or beef pieces to the dish, just put them in before adding any of the vegetables.

To make the curry sauce, heat the rapeseed oil in a large pan over a medium heat. Add the garlic and ginger and cook for 20 seconds or so, stirring. Tip in the onions and stir-fry for 5 minutes, until they are translucent but not coloured.

Pour the water into the pan and bring to the boil. Add the tomatoes, cumin, garam masala, paprika, turmeric and cayenne pepper, stirring well to combine. Season with salt and pepper and bring to the boil, then reduce to a simmer, cover and cook over a low heat for 30 minutes, until slightly reduced and thickened. Blitz with a hand-held blender until you have achieved a smooth sauce.

Add the cauliflower and chickpeas to the curry sauce, stirring well to combine. Reduce the heat, cover the pan with a lid and simmer for 8–10 minutes, until the cauliflower is just tender. Divide between shallow bowls and scatter over the coriander. Serve on plates with the coriander and garlic naan bread and natural yoghurt swirled with mango chutney on the side.

20 MINS

 25 MINS

 LOADS OF VEG

 FREEZER FRIENDLY

2 litres (3½ pints) chicken stock (from a cube is fine)

5 garlic cloves (3 peeled and 2 thinly sliced)

1 tbsp fresh thyme leaves

500g (1lb 2oz) potatoes, peeled and chopped

1 celeriac, peeled and chopped

100g (4oz) smoked bacon lardons

300ml (½ pint) cream

100ml (3½fl oz) unsweetened apple juice

2 tbsp rapeseed oil

sea salt and freshly ground black pepper

TO SERVE

buttered brown soda bread (optional)

Celeriac and Potato Soup with Smoked Bacon
Serves 4–6

Celeriac is the unsung hero of the vegetable world. This knobbly, odd-shaped root vegetable has a subtle celery flavour, with nutty overtones. It's now available in all supermarkets, but for some reason our nation isn't using it as much as we should. It makes an excellent velvety soup, but I also love using it in big-flavoured slow-cook dishes. It's available year round but is at its best from September to April, so it's the ideal vegetable to introduce yourself to if you aren't already familiar with it.

Place the stock, peeled garlic and half of the thyme in a large pan over a high heat. Add the potatoes, celeriac and half of the bacon and bring to the boil, then reduce the heat and simmer for 15–20 minutes, until all the vegetables are tender. Stir in most of the cream, reserving a little to garnish, along with all of the apple juice and use a hand-held blender to blitz until smooth. Season to taste with salt and pepper.

When almost ready to serve, heat the oil in a small frying pan and sauté the rest of the bacon lardons for a few minutes, until crisp and lightly golden. Stir in the sliced garlic with the rest of the thyme and cook for 30–60 seconds, until crisp.

Reheat the soup until warmed through, then ladle into warmed bowls and swirl in the remaining cream, then top with the smoked bacon and garlic mixture. Serve with buttered slices of brown soda bread, if liked.

CHAPTER 2 SUPERMARKET SWEEP

20 MINS

 LOADS OF VEG

Aromatic Chicken Salad with Satay Dressing
Serves 4-6

2 Little Gem lettuces

2 carrots, shredded into julienne

½ cucumber, halved, deseeded and cut into julienne

4 spring onions, trimmed and shredded

20g (¾oz) fresh coriander, leaves chopped

handful of fresh mint leaves, roughly torn

juice of 1 lime

1 rotisserie cooked chicken (about 600g (1lb 5oz) once removed from the bone)

2 tsp toasted sesame seeds

FOR THE SATAY DRESSING

3 tbsp peanut butter

2 tbsp boiling water

2 tbsp rapeseed oil

2 tbsp Sriracha chilli sauce

1 tbsp caster sugar

1 tbsp dark soy sauce

2 tsp rice wine vinegar

1 tsp balsamic vinegar

This is a great salad to make with a cooked chicken, which means it should take no more than 20 minutes to get on the table, particularly if you use a mandolin for the vegetables. The salad is full of fresh, spicy flavours that should perk up those taste buds.

To make the dressing, place the peanut butter in a bowl and whisk in the boiling water, then add the rest of the ingredients and continue to whisk until you have achieved a thick dressing. Set aside at room temperature until needed.

Separate the Little Gem lettuces into leaves, discarding any damaged outer leaves. Arrange on a large platter.

Place the carrots, cucumber and spring onions in a bowl, then add the coriander, mint and lime juice and toss until evenly combined. Add a small mound to each lettuce leaf.

Remove any skin from the chicken and finely shred the flesh. Place on top of the crunchy vegetable mixture and drizzle the peanut dressing on top. Sprinkle over the toasted sesame seeds to serve.

15 MINS

 15 MINS

 LOADS OF VEG

Sesame-Crusted Salmon with Pickled Carrot and Cucumber Salad Serves 4–6

1 heaped tbsp white sesame seeds

1 heaped tbsp black sesame seeds

4–6 × 150g (5oz) salmon fillets, skin on

2 tsp rapeseed oil

1 × 150g (5oz) packet of baby cucumbers

2 Little Gem lettuces, shredded

4 spring onions, finely chopped

20g (¾oz) fresh coriander, leaves stripped (and stalks discarded)

sea salt and freshly ground black pepper

FOR THE PICKLED CARROTS AND CHILLI

5 tbsp rice wine vinegar

5 tbsp water

1 tbsp caster sugar

4 carrots, peeled and julienned

1 fresh red chilli, deseeded and finely chopped

Although there are no carbs in this dish, salmon is a great protein to fill you up. If you are really short of time, pick up a couple packets of carrot spirals for ease or use daikon, which many supermarkets are now stocking – it's a long white radish regularly used in Japanese and Asian cooking.

Put the rice wine vinegar in a pan with the water and sugar. Add a pinch of salt and bring to a simmer. Put the carrots and chilli in a bowl, then pour the vinegar mixture on top. Set aside to pickle.

Meanwhile, place the black and white sesame seeds on a plate and mix well to combine. Press in each salmon fillet, skin side down, until evenly coated in the sesame seed mixture.

Heat the oil in a large non-stick frying pan over a medium heat. Add the salmon fillets and cook, skin side down, for 3 minutes. Turn over and cook for another 2 minutes or until cooked to your liking.

Pare the cucumbers into ribbons and put into a bowl with the lettuce, spring onions and coriander. Drain off the pickled carrot and chilli and add to the bowl along with a good grinding of pepper, then toss to lightly coat.

Arrange the salad on plates and add a piece of salmon alongside to serve.

20 MINS

 15 MINS

 LOADS OF VEG

Honeyed Duck with Five-Spice and Asian Salad
Serves 4-6

4 tbsp dark soy sauce

2 tbsp honey

½ tsp Chinese five-spice powder

4 × 200g (7oz) skinless duck breasts, sliced

1 tbsp rapeseed oil

1 red onion, thinly sliced

2 large carrots, peeled and cut into julienne

6 radishes, trimmed and thinly sliced

1 head of Chinese cabbage, halved, cored and finely shredded

1 bunch of spring onions, trimmed and cut into thin strips

1 tbsp white wine vinegar

2 tsp sesame oil

½ tsp caster sugar

good pinch of sea salt

TO GARNISH

fresh microgreens

TO SERVE

Thai fragrant rice

If you can't find skinless duck breasts, simply buy duck breasts with the skin on and remove it yourself or your butcher will be happy to do this for you. This recipe also works well with skinless chicken fillets, but you'll need to cook them initially for 3–4 minutes to ensure that they are cooked through.

Mix the soy sauce, honey and five-spice in a large bowl. Add the duck and toss until well coated. Set aside for 5 minutes to allow the flavours to develop.

Heat the oil in a wok or large frying pan over a medium to high heat. Lift the duck from the marinade (reserve the marinade) and stir-fry for 2–3 minutes, until browned all over. Pour over the reserved marinade and stir-fry for another 2–3 minutes, until slightly reduced and thickened. The duck should still be a little pink in the middle.

Place the red onion, carrots, radishes, Chinese cabbage and most of the spring onions in a bowl. Add the vinegar, sesame oil, sugar and salt, tossing well to coat.

Spoon the rice into bowls and garnish with the remaining spring onions, then add the honeyed duck with five-spice and Asian salad. Garnish with microgreens to serve.

25 MINS

 25 MINS

 FREEZER FRIENDLY

Pancetta Beef Burgers with Cheddar Shavings and Tarragon Mayonnaise Makes 6

2 tbsp milk

75g (3oz) fresh white ciabatta breadcrumbs

550g (1¼lb) premium steak mince (preferably rump)

1 garlic clove, crushed

2 tbsp chopped fresh flat-leaf parsley

1 tbsp tomato purée

1 tbsp Worcestershire sauce

6 slices of pancetta

6 sourdough burger buns

50g (2oz) rocket

175g (6oz) shop-bought tomato country relish

100g (4oz) mature Cheddar cheese

6 dill pickles

sea salt and freshly ground black pepper

FOR THE TARRAGON MAYONNAISE

150g (5oz) mayonnaise

1 tsp Dijon mustard

1 tbsp chopped fresh tarragon

These burgers are royal in the true sense of the word and their success depends on good-quality ingredients. Choose a premium steak mince – I really like rump – and make sure it's nice and fresh with a good red colour.

First make the tarragon mayonnaise. Place the mayonnaise, mustard and tarragon in a bowl and season with salt and pepper. Mix well to combine, then chill until needed.

To make the burgers, put the milk in a large bowl with the breadcrumbs and set aside for 5 minutes to allow the breadcrumbs to absorb the milk. Add the steak mince, garlic, parsley, tomato purée and Worcestershire sauce and season with salt and pepper. Using your hands, mix well to combine. Shape into six patties.

Heat a large non-stick frying or griddle pan over a medium-high heat. Add the patties and cook for 4 minutes on each side or until cooked to your liking – you may have to do this in batches depending on the size of your pan. Remove to a plate and leave to rest. Add the pancetta to the pan and cook for 1 minute on each side, until lightly golden.

Split the buns and lightly toast under the grill, then spread with the tarragon mayonnaise. Arrange a small pile of rocket on the bottom of each one. Top with a beef burger, a slice of pancetta and a dollop of tomato country relish. Using a vegetable peeler, pare over shavings of Cheddar and dill pickles. Add the tops of the buns and serve at once with the rest of the rocket as a salad on the side.

15 MINS

 25 MINS

 LOADS OF VEG

Bacon, Egg and Bean Bowl
Serves 4–6

1 ciabatta loaf, cut or torn into bite-sized pieces

6 back bacon rashers (dry-cured if possible)

150ml (¼ pint) rapeseed oil

6 eggs

200g (7oz) French beans, trimmed and halved

1 large Cos lettuce

1 bunch of spring onions, trimmed and thinly sliced on the diagonal

300g (11oz) cherry tomatoes on the vine, halved

2 tbsp white wine vinegar

4 tsp Dijon mustard

sea salt and freshly ground black pepper

These salad bowls are so simple to pull together with very little effort and you would get all the ingredients in any small supermarket. Perfect when you're hungry but don't feel like cooking a large meal and the added bonus is that there's very little washing up.

Preheat the oven to 180°C (350°F/gas mark 4).

Put the ciabatta and bacon rashers on a baking tray and drizzle with 4 tablespoons of the oil, then season the bread with salt and pepper. Bake in the preheated oven for 15 minutes, until the bread is crisp and golden and the bacon is sizzling and tender, turning halfway through. Roughly chop the bacon and set both aside until needed.

Meanwhile, put the eggs in a pan of cold water and bring to the boil, then reduce the heat to medium and simmer for 6 minutes. Add the French beans after 2 minutes. Drain in a colander and quickly refresh to prevent the beans from cooking any further. Crack the shells off the eggs and peel, then cut into quarters.

Tear the lettuce into a big bowl, then add the spring onions, tomatoes, French beans and ciabatta croutons.

Mix the remaining 6 tablespoons of the oil with the vinegar and mustard in a screw-topped jar. Season with salt and pepper and shake until thickened and emulsified. Drizzle over the salad, tossing gently to coat.

Divide the salad between bowls and arrange the bacon and eggs on top to serve.

20 MINS

 30 MINS

 LOADS OF VEG

Crispy Lamb Chops with Cauliflower and Leek Purée
Serves 4–6

75g (3oz) panko breadcrumbs

50g (2oz) Parma ham, very finely chopped

5 tbsp freshly grated Parmesan cheese

1 tbsp chopped fresh flat-leaf parsley

4–6 boneless lamb chops (or 8–12 cutlets)

2 eggs

4 tbsp rapeseed oil

sea salt and freshly ground black pepper

FOR THE CAULIFLOWER
AND LEEK PURÉE

25g (1oz) butter

120ml (4fl oz) chicken or vegetable stock (from a cube is fine)

1 cauliflower, trimmed and broken into small florets

4 leeks, trimmed and finely sliced

6 tbsp cream

TO SERVE

steamed French beans

redcurrant jelly

Try to buy Connemara Hill lamb for this recipe, one of the most exciting uniquely Irish products on the market. The lambs eat a diet of wild herbs, flowers and heathers to give the meat a special flavour. Happily, Dunnes Stores now supplies it when it's in season, so keep an eye out for it in the Simply Better range.

Tip the breadcrumbs into a bowl and mix in the Parma ham, Parmesan and parsley. Season generously with freshly ground black pepper, then mix really well. Tip into a shallow dish.

Trim any excess fat off the chops or cutlets, then beat a little bit with a meat tenderiser or a rolling pin (a frying pan would also do the job). Beat the eggs in a separate dish and season generously, then use to coat the chops or cutlets. Cover with the breadcrumb mixture, ensuring they are each evenly coated. Set aside.

To make the cauliflower and leek purée, bring the butter and stock to the boil in a pan with a lid until it forms an emulsion. Add the cauliflower florets with a good pinch of salt, cover the pan and cook for 6–8 minutes, until tender. Tip in the leeks and cook for another 3–4 minutes, stirring occasionally, until just tender but still a vibrant green colour. Add the cream and blitz with a hand-held blender until smooth, then season generously with pepper.

Heat the oil in a large heavy-based frying pan over a medium heat. Add the coated chops and cook for 3–4 minutes on each side for large chops or 1–2 minutes on each side if using cutlets. They should be crisp on the outside but still pink in the middle. Transfer to a plate lined with kitchen paper to absorb any excess oil.

Meanwhile, gently reheat the cauliflower and leek purée and divide between warmed serving plates. Add the crispy chops and French beans with a dollop of redcurrant jelly to serve.

15 MINS

 20 MINS

Sticky Pork and Pineapple Skewers with Mango Salsa
Serves 4–6

4 tbsp dark soy sauce

2 tsp mild curry seasoning or curry powder (I love the Dunnes Stores Simply Better Mild Curry Seasoning)

500g (1lb 2oz) boneless pork fillet, trimmed and cut into long strips

250g (9oz) fresh pineapple chunks (from a carton is perfect)

2 Little Gem lettuces

freshly ground black pepper

FOR THE MANGO SALSA

1 small red onion, finely diced

juice of 1 lime

pinch of caster sugar

1 small ripe mango, peeled and diced

1 spring onion, finely chopped

1 fresh mild green chilli, deseeded and finely chopped

handful of fresh mint leaves

A quick and satisfying supper of sticky pork skewers intertwined with pineapple chunks and mango salsa that is packed full of flavour and colour. When the skewers are cooked, the juice of the pineapple helps to form a lovely sticky glaze that is delicious.

Preheat a griddle pan until it's smoking hot.

Whisk together the soy sauce and curry seasoning or powder and season with pepper, then stir in the pork strips. Leave to marinate for 2 minutes, then thread the pork pieces onto 8–12 × 15cm (6in) bamboo skewers with the pineapple chunks and arrange on the griddle pan.

Reduce the heat to medium, then add the pork and pineapple skewers to the pan and cook for 10–12 minutes, turning once or twice, until completely tender and cooked through.

Meanwhile, to make the mango salsa, place the red onion in a medium-sized bowl with the lime juice and sugar. Set aside to pickle for 5 minutes, then stir in the mango, spring onion and chilli. Tear in the mint leaves and gently fold together to combine. .

Tear the Little Gem lettuce leaves and divide between plates. Spoon over the mango salsa, then arrange the sticky pork and pineapple skewers alongside to serve.

15 MINS

 25 MINS

 LOADS OF VEG

Vegetable Pizza with Burrata and Rocket
Makes 4 large pizzas

1 tbsp rapeseed oil

2 red onions, thinly sliced

2 red peppers, thinly sliced

300g (11oz) chestnut mushrooms, sliced

4 ready-made stone-baked pizza bases (such as Pizza da Piero)

225g (8oz) passata (from a jar or carton)

2 × 125g (4½oz) balls of burrata cheese

4 tbsp freshly grated Parmesan cheese

50g (2oz) rocket

sea salt and freshly ground black pepper

TO SERVE

mixed side salad (optional)

Burrata cheese takes the delicious mozzarella cheese that we have embraced as a nation one step further – it's mozzarella that is formed into a pouch and then filled with soft, stringy curd and cream.

Preheat the oven to 200°C (400°F/gas mark 6).

Heat the oil in a sauté pan over a medium heat. Add the onions and peppers and cook for 2–3 minutes, until softened. Add the mushrooms, season with salt and pepper and cook for another minute or two.

Spread the pizza bases with the passata and arrange the vegetables on top. Tear over the burrata and sprinkle with the Parmesan. Place in the preheated oven directly on the oven shelf and cook for 10–12 minutes, until piping hot and golden – you'll need to do this in batches.

Transfer back onto the chopping board and scatter over the rocket, then cut into slices. Arrange on plates with a mixed side salad, if liked, to serve.

20 MINS

 30 MINS

❄ FREEZER FRIENDLY (MEAT)

1 tbsp rapeseed oil

50g (2oz) raw chorizo, diced

350g (12oz) lean minced beef

1 small onion, finely chopped

1 green pepper, diced

1 fresh small green chilli, deseeded and finely chopped (optional)

140g (4¾oz) tomato purée

3 tbsp dark brown muscovado sugar

2 tbsp apple cider vinegar

1 tbsp honey

2 tsp Dijon mustard

1 tsp Worcestershire sauce

1 × 400g (14oz) tin of kidney beans in chilli sauce

4–6 burger buns

1 Little Gem lettuce, shredded

100g (4oz) Cheddar cheese, grated

handful of mixed hot chillies in brine or sliced jalapeño chillies, drained (optional)

sea salt and freshly ground black pepper

American-Style Sloppy Joes
Serves 4–6

This is a version of a sandwich that is an all-American classic, consisting of minced beef cooked in a spicy tomato sauce, often with the addition of kidney beans. It should be a hit with all the family and is very quick to prepare. According to legend, a cook named Joe at Floyd Angell's café in Sioux City, Iowa, added tomato sauce to his 'loose meat' sandwiches and the 'sloppy Joe' sandwich was born. The rest, as they say, is history!

Heat the oil in a large sauté pan over a medium heat. Add the chorizo and cook until it just starts to release its oil, then add the minced beef. Stir-fry until the meat starts to brown, breaking up any lumps with a wooden spoon. Add the onion, green pepper and chilli (if using) and continue to cook for another 5 minutes or so, until the vegetables are beginning to soften.

Add the tomato purée, sugar, vinegar, honey, mustard and Worcestershire sauce and stir until well combined, then stir in the beans. Season to taste, then bring to a simmer and cook for another 15 minutes, stirring occasionally, until the sauce is nice and thick.

Toast the burger buns under the grill. Arrange the lettuce on the bottom of each bun, then spoon over the sloppy Joe beef mixture. Scatter the grated Cheddar on top with the hot chillies (if using), then sandwich together with the tops of the buns.

20 MINS

 40 MINS

Pan-Fried Trout with Kale, Shallots and Potatoes
Serves 4–6

4–6 × 150–175g (5–6oz) fresh trout fillets, skinned and boned

50g (2oz) butter

500g (1lb 2oz) potatoes, peeled and cut into bite-sized pieces

2 tbsp rapeseed oil

450g (1lb) small shallots, peeled and halved if large

4 tbsp chicken stock (from a cube is fine)

350g (12oz) kale, stems removed and leaves roughly chopped

sea salt and freshly ground black pepper

TO SERVE

lemon wedges

While I've used trout fillets, you could certainly use any other kind of fish in this recipe. The trout is nice because the fillets are so thin that they take just minutes to cook. A thicker fish would obviously take more time to cook through.

Preheat the grill to medium-high.

Arrange the trout fillets on a baking tray lined with non-stick baking paper. Season with salt and pepper, then dot with 25g (1oz) of the butter. Place under the grill and cook for 5–7 minutes, until tender and cooked through. Keep warm.

Meanwhile, place the potatoes in a pan of cold salted water over a high heat. Bring to the boil and cook for 5 minutes, until partially cooked. Drain and set aside.

Heat the remaining butter with the oil in a large non-stick frying pan over a medium heat. Add the potatoes, then season with salt and pepper and sauté for 10 minutes, stirring occasionally. Add the shallots and sprinkle over the stock, then sauté for another 5 minutes, until the shallots are golden and the potatoes are tender.

Increase the heat to high, add the kale and sauté for another 3–4 minutes, until the kale is tender and just crisp around the edges.

Arrange the grilled trout on plates with the kale, shallots and potatoes and garnish each one with a lemon wedge to serve.

15 MINS

 15 MINS

❄ FREEZER FRIENDLY (SKEWERS)

Piri Piri Prawn and Chorizo Skewers with Chargrilled Little Gem Wedges Serves 4–6

4 Little Gem lettuces, each one trimmed and cut into 6 wedges

2 uncooked chorizo sausages (each about 100g (4oz))

2 × 200g (7oz) packets of wild Atlantic jumbo prawns, peeled and with tails still intact

FOR THE PIRI PIRI SAUCE

2 long fresh red chillies, deseeded and roughly chopped

2 garlic cloves, roughly chopped

6 tbsp lemon juice

6 tbsp rapeseed oil, plus a little extra for brushing

2 tsp caster sugar

1 tsp paprika

½ tsp cayenne pepper

sea salt and freshly ground black pepper

TO SERVE

2 lemons, cut into wedges

Choose wild Atlantic jumbo prawns for this recipe, as they need to be large enough to wrap around the slices of chorizo. Of course you could also cook this on the barbecue if the weather is fine.

To make the piri piri sauce, place the chillies, garlic, lemon juice, rapeseed oil, sugar, paprika and cayenne pepper in a small food processor and season generously with salt and pepper. Blitz until you have achieved a coarse paste. Using a spatula, transfer to a bowl. Set aside until needed.

Heat a griddle pan over a medium to high heat. Brush the Little Gem lettuce wedges lightly with rapeseed oil and quickly chargrill. Arrange the wedges on plates and add a small dipping bowl of the piri piri sauce.

Cut the chorizo sausages into 24 even-sized slices, discarding the ends. Wrap each prawn around a slice of chorizo and thread two prawns onto each skewer. Brush all over with the remaining piri piri sauce and cook the skewers on the griddle pan in batches over a medium heat for 2–3 minutes on each side, until the prawns and chorizo are cooked through and tender.

Add the prawn and chorizo skewers to the plates with the Little Gem wedges and lemon wedges to serve.

15 MINS

 20 MINS

 LOADS OF VEG

Smoked Haddock with Tenderstem Broccoli, Spinach and Conchiglie Serves 4–6

2 tbsp rapeseed oil

6 rindless smoked streaky bacon rashers, chopped

2 garlic cloves, finely chopped

500g (1lb 2oz) conchiglie (pasta shells)

2 × 200g (7oz) packets of tenderstem broccoli (or purple sprouting broccoli if in season), halved

300ml (½ pint) cream

1 heaped tbsp wholegrain mustard

450g (1lb) smoked haddock, skinned and cut into bite-sized pieces (undyed if possible)

150g (5oz) baby spinach

pared rind and juice of 1 lemon

20g (¾oz) fresh chives, snipped

sea salt and freshly ground black pepper

Look for traditional, undyed smoked haddock, which is naturally off-white and pale yellow, or if you have a good fishmonger you might also come across smoked cod. The flavour of this is worlds apart from the more common bright yellow smoked haddock, which has far too strong a flavour for many people's tastes.

Heat the oil in a frying pan over a high heat. Add the bacon and sauté for 2 minutes, then add the garlic and cook for another minute or so, until the bacon is crisp.

Cook the pasta in a large pan of boiling salted water for 10–12 minutes or according to the packet instructions, until al dente (tender but still with a bite). Three minutes before the end of the cooking time, add the tenderstem broccoli to the pan.

Meanwhile, stir the cream and mustard into the bacon mixture, then stir in the haddock and cook over a medium heat for 2 minutes. Fold in the spinach and cook for another minute or so, until the smoked haddock is cooked through and opaque.

Drain the pasta and broccoli and return to the pan, then fold in the haddock and spinach mixture. Add lemon juice to taste, then stir in the chives. Toss together and season lightly with salt and plenty of pepper. Divide between bowls and scatter over the lemon rind to serve.

15 MINS

 20 MINS

 LOADS OF VEG

Seared Salmon with Pea and Watercress Purée
Serves 4–6

4–6 × 150g (5oz) salmon fillets, skin on (scaled), organic if possible

1 tbsp rapeseed oil, plus extra for brushing

25g (1oz) butter

sea salt and freshly ground black pepper

FOR THE PEA AND WATERCRESS PURÉE

500g (1lb 2oz) frozen peas

1 heaped tbsp chopped fresh mint (stalks removed and reserved)

100g (4oz) watercress

4 tbsp crème fraîche

TO GARNISH

microgreens (optional)

TO SERVE

seasonal vegetables

Organic Irish salmon is a great option as a sustainable fish and the fatty acids in oily fish such as salmon have significant health benefits. It all comes from the pristine waters along Ireland's exposed westerly coastline, so the fish have a good firm texture and represent excellent value for money.

Lightly score the salmon skin four or five times diagonally, taking care not to cut into the flesh. Brush the skin with oil and season with salt and pepper.

Heat the butter and oil in a large frying pan over a medium to high heat. Add the salmon, skin side down, in one layer. Cook for 6–7 minutes, until the skin is crisp. Cover with a lid for 2–3 minutes to ensure the top of the fish is cooked through if necessary or carefully turn over and cook flesh side down for another 1–2 minutes, until just cooked through and tender.

Meanwhile, bring a large pan of salted water to the boil. Add the peas and mint stalks and cook for 3 minutes. Drain, reserving a cup of the water. Discard the mint stalks.

Return the peas to the pan and, using a hand-held blender, blitz with the watercress and mint leaves to a coarse purée (you can also do this in a food processor). Add the crème fraîche and a little of the reserved pea water if necessary to loosen the mixture.

Divide the pea and watercress purée between plates and top with the salmon, skin side up. Garnish with the microgreens (if using) and serve with seasonal vegetables.

20 MINS + 15 MINS RESTING

1 HR

Speedy Roast Chicken with Potato Wedges and Romesco Sauce Serves 4-6

3 tbsp rapeseed oil

1 tsp smoked paprika

½ tsp chopped fresh thyme, plus extra sprigs to garnish

1 spatchcock chicken (preferably free-range or organic)

4 large baking potatoes, peeled and cut into wedges

2 large garlic bulbs, halved

300ml (½ pint) chicken stock (from a cube is fine)

1 small lemon, sliced

sea salt and freshly ground black pepper

FOR THE ROMESCO SAUCE

2 garlic cloves, peeled

1 × 340g (12oz) jar of roasted peppers in brine, drained

100g (4oz) toasted blanched almonds

2 tbsp red wine vinegar

1 tbsp rapeseed oil

I'm sure you've seen spatchcock chickens in the supermarkets and many are already flavoured, but if you want to do your own, it's really very easy. Using a kitchen shears or sharp knife, cut the chicken along both sides of the backbone to remove it, then just flip the chicken over and press it down on the breastbone until you hear it crack.

Preheat the oven to 200°C (400°F/gas mark 6).

Mix the oil with the paprika and thyme. Rub the chicken all over with some of the oil mixture and season with salt and pepper, then tuck the wings slightly under the breast.

Put the potato wedges and halved garlic bulbs into a large roasting tin and toss in the remaining oil mixture, then pour around the chicken stock and add the lemon slices.

Place the chicken on a rack set in the roasting tin and roast on the middle shelf of the preheated oven for 45 minutes, until the skin is nice and crisp and the flesh is cooked through and tender.

Meanwhile, to make the romesco sauce, place the peeled garlic cloves in a food processor with the entire drained contents of the jar of roasted peppers and the almonds, vinegar and oil. Blend until smooth, then transfer to a bowl and season with salt and pepper.

Transfer the cooked chicken to a carving board and loosely cover with foil. Leave to rest for about 15 minutes. Give the potatoes a quick shake to even them out, then return to the oven while the chicken is resting.

Once the chicken has rested, chop into pieces and arrange on plates with bowls of the romesco sauce, potato wedges and some of the roasted garlic, if liked. Garnish with a few sprigs of thyme to serve.

25 MINS + 1 HR DRAINING

 20 MINS

 LOADS OF VEG

 FREEZER FRIENDLY (BURGERS)

2 red dessert apples

800g (1¾lb) lean minced pork

2 tsp paprika

1 tbsp rapeseed oil

150g (5oz) Wicklow Blue cheese, sliced

6 blaa or burger buns, split in half

4 tbsp caramelised red onion chutney

50g (2oz) baby salad leaves

sea salt and freshly ground black pepper

FOR THE WINTER COLESLAW

½ celeriac, peeled

¼ red cabbage, tough core removed

2 carrots, peeled

2 tsp caster sugar

5 tbsp mayonnaise

1 tbsp Dijon mustard

1 tbsp white wine vinegar

Pork and Apple Burgers with Wicklow Blue Cheese and Winter Coleslaw Makes 6

This winter slaw is very versatile and can be served with all types of things. It's best with the mayonnaise mixed in just before serving, but leftovers are still good if kept covered in the fridge for up to two days. The combination goes beautifully with the pork and blue cheese, spiked with a little sweetness from the apple.

To make the winter slaw, use the grating attachment of a food processor or the coarse side of an ordinary box grater to grate the celeriac, red cabbage and carrots. Sprinkle over the sugar and 1 teaspoon of salt. Make sure it's well mixed, then place into a colander set in the sink. Leave to drain for at least 1 hour to remove the excess liquid.

Meanwhile, cut the apple into quarters, remove the core and grate the flesh into a bowl with the minced pork and paprika. Season with salt and pepper and mix well with your hands. Shape into six round patties, flattening them slightly.

Heat a griddle pan over a medium-high heat. Brush the burgers with the oil and add to the hot pan. Reduce the heat to medium and cook for 5–6 minutes on each side, until lightly browned and cooked through. Turn off the heat, lay the cheese on top of the burgers and leave to rest.

Give the grated vegetables a good squeeze before placing in a large bowl. Mix the mayonnaise, mustard and vinegar in a small bowl, then fold into the grated vegetables until evenly coated. Season to taste with salt and pepper.

Toast the buns on a grill rack under a medium heat until lightly toasted. Add a little of the coleslaw, then cover with a burger topped with the blue cheese and finish with a dollop of the chuntey and a small mound of baby salad leaves. Place the burger bun tops to the side and serve the rest of the winter slaw alongside.

20 MINS

 15 MINS

 FREEZER FRIENDLY (PORK)

75g (3oz) butter

150g (5oz) fresh ciabatta breadcrumbs

2 tsp fresh thyme leaves

20g (¾oz) fresh flat-leaf parsley, leaves stripped and finely chopped

1 tbsp rapeseed oil

500g (1lb 2oz) pork fillet, well trimmed and thinly sliced on the diagonal into schnitzel-style steaks

sea salt and freshly ground black pepper

FOR THE FENNEL SLAW

2 fennel bulbs

20g (¾oz) fresh chives, finely chopped

4 tbsp mayonnaise

juice of 1 small lemon, plus extra wedges to serve

1 tsp Dijon mustard

Crispy Pork Schnitzel with Fennel Slaw
Serves 4-6

Some supermarkets sell thinly sliced pork escalopes, which are also perfect to use in this dish. The trick is to get a good colour underneath before you flash them under the grill.

Preheat the grill to medium-hot.

Melt the butter in a large ovenproof frying pan over a medium heat, then stir in the breadcrumbs, thyme and 1 tablespoon of the chopped parsley and season with salt and pepper. Tip out onto a plate and wipe out the pan.

Put the pan back on a medium to high heat. Add the oil, then add the pork steaks and cook for 3–4 minutes, until nicely browned. Turn over and sprinkle on the prepared breadcrumbs, then place under the grill for another 3–4 minutes, until golden brown and cooked through.

Meanwhile, make the fennel slaw. Thinly slice the fennel bulbs – a mandolin works brilliantly for this – and place in a large bowl. Add the rest of the parsley and the chives. Fold in the mayonnaise with the lemon juice and mustard until evenly combined, adding a couple of drops of water if you think the dressing needs thinning out.

Arrange the pork schnitzels on plates with the fennel slaw and serve with the lemon wedges.

15 MINS

 20 MINS

Linguine with Prawns, Peas and Fine Beans
Serves 4–6

500g (1lb 2oz) linguine

175g (6oz) frozen peas

200g (7oz) fine green beans, trimmed and halved

450g (1lb) cooked black tiger prawns

finely grated rind and juice of 1 small lemon

300ml (½ pint) crème fraîche

20g (¾oz) fresh flat-leaf parsley, leaves stripped and roughly chopped

20g (¾oz) fresh basil, leaves stripped and shredded

sea salt and freshly ground black pepper

A super-easy dish that only uses one pot and the herbs really help to lift the flavours of the vegetables and prawns into a lovely flavourful dish.

Cook the pasta in a large pan of boiling salted water for 10–12 minutes or according to the packet instructions, until al dente (tender but still with a bite). Four minutes before the end of the cooking time, add the frozen peas and green beans to the pan.

Drain the pasta and vegetables, then return to the pan over a low heat. Add the prawns, lemon rind and juice, crème fraîche and the herbs. Season to taste with salt and pepper and heat through for 4–5 minutes, until the sauce is slightly reduced and piping hot.

Divide between bowls and add a good grinding of black pepper to each one before serving.

15 MINS

 15 MINS

 FREEZER FRIENDLY

Stir-Fried Beef and Mushrooms with Kale and Black Bean Sauce
Serves 4-6

2 tbsp dark soy sauce

2 tbsp oyster sauce

4 tsp cornflour

700g (1lb 9oz) rump steak, trimmed and cut into strips

3 tbsp rapeseed oil

250g (9oz) curly kale, tough stalks trimmed and roughly shredded

200g (7oz) chestnut mushrooms, sliced

250ml (9fl oz) vegetable stock (from a cube is fine)

4 tbsp black bean sauce

TO SERVE

boiled rice

A quick and easy way to give kale a nice Oriental kick. Curly kale is one of those vegetables that's so good for you, but people often ask me what the best way to cook it so that the whole family will eat it. This stir-fry is the perfect answer.

Place the soy and oyster sauce in a shallow dish with the cornflour and mix well to combine. Add the steak strips, stirring to combine, and set aside for 10 minutes to allow the flavours to develop if time allows.

Heat a wok or large non-stick frying pan over a high heat. Add half the oil, swirling it up the sides of the wok, then add the steak and stir-fry for 3-4 minutes, until browned – you may need to do this in two batches depending on the size of your wok or pan. Tip into a bowl and set aside.

Wipe out the wok and put it back on a high heat. Add the rest of the oil, tip in the kale and mushrooms and season to taste with salt and pepper. Stir-fry for 2 minutes. Pour in the stock and cook, uncovered, for 2-3 minutes, stirring occasionally, until all the stock has been absorbed.

Return the steak to the wok with the black bean sauce and toss together for a minute or two until heated through. Spoon into bowls with boiled rice.

15 MINS

 45 MINS

 LOADS OF VEG

 FREEZER FRIENDLY

1 × 290g (10¼oz) jar of sun-dried tomatoes

4–6 boneless, skin-on corn-fed chicken fillets

1 large onion, finely chopped

2 garlic cloves, crushed

100g (4oz) raw chorizo, peeled and sliced

1½ tsp herbs de Provence

500g (1lb 2oz) long grain rice

150ml (¼ pint) dry white wine

1 × 400g (14oz) tin of Italian chopped tomatoes

600ml (1 pint) chicken stock (from a cube is fine)

sea salt and freshly ground black pepper

TO GARNISH

chopped fresh flat-leaf parsley

Braised Chicken and Chorizo Rice Serves 4–6

Once you've got this cooking, you can leave it and get on with other things. It's so delicious on a cold night when you are late in from work. The sun-dried tomatoes and chorizo conjure up memories of summer holidays and give wonderful depth of flavour with very little effort on your part – my kind of cooking!

Preheat the oven to 180°C (350°F/gas mark 4).

Drain and reserve the oil from the sun-dried tomatoes and finely chop, then set aside.

Add 2 tablespoons of the reserved oil to a heavy-based casserole with a lid. Season the chicken, then add to the casserole, skin side down, and cook for 2–3 minutes, until lightly browned. Transfer to a plate and set aside.

Add the onion and garlic and sauté for 2–3 minutes, then add the chorizo, sun-dried tomatoes and herbs and cook for another 2 minutes. Add the rice and stir until well coated, then pour the wine into the casserole, stirring to remove any browned bits from the bottom. Add the tomatoes and stock, then season with salt and pepper. Arrange the chicken on top, pushing the fillets down into the rice. Cover the casserole with a lid, transfer to the oven and cook for 20–25 minutes, until all the liquid has been absorbed and the chicken and rice are cooked through and tender.

Scatter over the parsley, then leave to stand for 5 minutes. Remove the lid and gently fluff up the rice with a fork. Serve straight to the table.

20 MINS

 30 MINS

 FREEZER FRIENDLY (CAKES)

150g (5oz) plain flour

6–8 large eggs

100ml (3½fl oz) buttermilk

400g (14oz) sweet potatoes, peeled and grated

1 bunch of spring onions, finely chopped

1 fresh red chilli, deseeded and finely chopped

200g (7oz) feta cheese, crumbled

rapeseed oil, for frying

225g (8oz) dry-cure streaky bacon rashers

2 ripe avocados

sea salt and freshly ground black pepper

Sweet Potato Cakes with Crispy Bacon, Smashed Avocado and Poached Eggs Serves 4–6

My twins love these sweet potato cakes as a speedy supper and I often just serve them with some nice steamed green vegetables, but with crispy bacon, smashed avocado and poached eggs it becomes a brunch-inspired dish that makes a fantastic midweek meal.

Sieve the flour into a large bowl, break in two of the eggs and add the buttermilk. Slowly whisk together to combine. Add the grated sweet potatoes, spring onions, chilli and 75g (3oz) of the feta. Season with plenty of pepper and a small pinch of salt, as the feta is already quite salty. Using a spatula, mix until well combined.

Pour about 1cm (¼in) of oil into a large non-stick frying pan and place over a medium heat. Working in batches, place four separate heaped spoonfuls of the sweet potato mixture into the pan and gently flatten down each one with the back of the spatula. Fry the sweet potato cakes for 3–4 minutes on each side, until golden brown. Keep warm in a low oven.

Meanwhile, grill the bacon on the grill pan under a medium-high heat for 3–4 minutes, turning once.

Bring a large pan of water to the boil and poach the remaining eggs for 2–3 minutes, until the whites are firm but the yolks are still soft.

Cut the avocados in half and scoop the flesh in a bowl. Roughly smash with a fork and season with salt and pepper.

Arrange the sweet potato cakes on plates and top with the bacon, smashed avocado and poached eggs, then scatter over the rest of the feta to serve.

20 MINS

 20 MINS

Porcini Salted Steak with Chestnut Mushrooms on Sourdough Serves 4–6

1 cob loaf of sourdough bread, cut into 4–6 even-sized slices (ends discarded)

1 tbsp rapeseed oil

4–6 × 100g (4oz) fillet steaks

25g (1oz) butter

250g (9oz) chestnut mushrooms, quartered

25g (1oz) lamb's lettuce

sea salt and freshly ground black pepper

FOR THE PORCINI SALT

1 tsp fresh thyme leaves, very finely chopped

1 tsp sea salt flakes

½ tsp ground dried porcini mushrooms (ground to a powder in a spice or coffee grinder)

FOR THE HORSERADISH MAYONNAISE

4 tbsp mayonnaise

2 tsp horseradish cream

1 tsp Dijon mustard

Ground dried porcini mushrooms have a robust, nutty, concentrated mushroom flavour that makes a brilliant seasoning for steaks. It's also a wonderful seasoning for any grilled vegetables, so make up a big batch for the barbecue season and you'll find yourself using it a lot.

To make the porcini salt, place the thyme, salt and ground dried mushrooms in a bowl, mixing to combine.

To make the horseradish mayonnaise, place the mayonnaise, horseradish cream and mustard in a bowl, season with salt and pepper and stir to combine.

Heat a griddle pan over a medium to high heat. Brush the bread with some of the oil and add it to the griddle pan. Cook in batches for 1–2 minutes on each side, until lightly charred. Set aside on a plate.

Brush the steaks with the rest of the oil and sprinkle over most of the porcini salt. Add to the hot griddle pan and cook for 1 minute, then turn the steaks over and cook for another 3–4 minutes, until rare (cook the steaks for a little longer if you like your meat more well done). Leave to rest for 3–4 minutes, then thinly slice.

Melt the butter, then tip in the mushrooms and season with salt and pepper. Sauté for 4–5 minutes, until cooked through and tender.

Spread the slices of sourdough with the horseradish mayonnaise and top each one with strips of the steak. Add the mushrooms and sprinkle the rest of the porcini salt on top. Scatter over the lamb's lettuce and arrange on warmed plates to serve.

30 MINS

 30 MINS

Steak with Peppercorn Sauce and Rustic Potato Slices Serves 4-6

4-6 × 150–175g (5–6oz) striploin or sirloin steaks, well trimmed and at room temperature

rapeseed oil, for brushing

sea salt and freshly ground black pepper

FOR THE RUSTIC POTATO SLICES

675g (1½lb) potatoes, scraped or scrubbed clean

1 fresh rosemary sprig, broken into tiny sprigs

3 garlic cloves, lightly crushed (skin still on)

3 tbsp rapeseed oil

FOR THE PEPPERCORN SAUCE

15g (½oz) butter

2 shallots, finely chopped

2 garlic cloves, crushed

450ml (¾ pint) beef stock (from a cube is fine)

2 tsp crushed black peppercorns

4 tbsp cream

2 tbsp Cognac

TO SERVE

sautéed Savoy cabbage

These ultra-trendy potato slices not only go well with steak, but are fantastic as a side dish for a barbecue. They can be made in large quantities in trays and simply reheated as necessary.

Preheat the oven to 200°C (400°F/gas mark 6).

Cut the potatoes into slices 5mm (¼in) thick and arrange in a single layer in a roasting tin lined with non-stick baking paper. Add the rosemary and garlic and season generously with salt. Drizzle over the oil and toss until evenly coated. Roast in the preheated oven for 15–20 minutes, until cooked through and lightly golden, turning once or twice.

Meanwhile, to make the peppercorn sauce, melt the butter in a pan over a medium heat. Add the shallots and garlic and cook for 3–4 minutes, until softened but not coloured. Stir in the stock and cook for 10–15 minutes, until reduced by half. Strain the sauce into a clean pan, discarding the shallots and garlic. Add the crushed peppercorns, cream and Cognac and season with salt. Cook for 2–3 minutes, until slightly reduced and thickened. Keep warm.

Heat a griddle pan over a high heat. Brush the steaks with oil and season with salt and pepper. Cook for 3 minutes on each side for medium-rare or until cooked to your liking.

Serve the steaks with sautéed Savoy cabbage, potato slices and peppercorn sauce.

15 MINS

 15 MINS

 FREEZER FRIENDLY

Turkish Pizza with Spiced Minced Lamb
Makes 4 large pizzas

400g (14oz) lean minced lamb

1 red onion, very finely chopped

20g (¾oz) fresh flat-leaf parsley, leaves stripped and finely chopped

1 tbsp honey

1 tsp ground cinnamon

1 tsp ground allspice

1 tsp dried chilli flakes

4 ready-made thin pizza bases (such as Pizza da Piero)

rapeseed oil, for brushing

4 tbsp light tahini (sesame seed paste)

4 tbsp pine nuts

sea salt and freshly ground black pepper

TO SERVE

tomato, radish and cucumber salad (optional – see the intro)

These pizzas are so delicious and are served all over Turkey. Once you've tasted them, it's not difficult to see why! I like to top them with a salad made from diced cucumber and tomatoes mixed with thinly sliced radishes along with some roughly chopped dill, then simply dress with a little oil and lemon juice before serving.

Preheat the oven to 220°C (425°F/gas mark 7). Line four baking sheets with non-stick baking paper (or work in batches, making two pizzas at a time).

To make the lamb topping, put the minced lamb in a bowl and season generously with salt and pepper, then add the onion, parsley, honey and spices and mix well to combine.

Place each pizza base on a lined baking sheet, brush with a little oil and spread a thin layer of tahini on each one.

Divide the filling into four and spread it evenly on top of the pizzas. Bake in the preheated oven for 15 minutes, then scatter over the pine nuts and bake for 5 minutes more, until the pizzas are cooked through and the edges are golden brown.

Remove the cooked pizzas from the oven and transfer to large flat plates, then spoon the salad on top (if using) to serve.

10 MINS

 20 MINS

 LOADS OF VEG

500g (1lb 2oz) penne pasta

50g (2oz) pine nuts

6 premium pork sausages (such as James Whelan's sun-dried tomato and basil)

2 tbsp rapeseed oil

1 bunch of cavolo nero, trimmed and shredded

100g (4oz) freshly grated Parmesan cheese

sea salt and freshly ground black pepper

Instant Meatballs with Cavolo Nero and Penne
Serves 4–6

Cavolo nero is a variety of Italian kale that grows very successfully in Ireland, so it's becoming much more commonplace on our supermarket shelves. It's packed full of nutrients and flavour and many people who don't enjoy regular kale can be won over by this variety.

Cook the pasta in a large pan of boiling salted water for 10–12 minutes, until al dente (tender but still with a little bite).

Heat a large sauté pan over a high heat and toast the pine nuts, tossing them constantly to ensure they don't burn. Tip onto a plate.

Squeeze the sausages from their skins and roughly break into 24 pieces. Roll into balls.

Heat the oil in the same sauté pan over a medium heat. Add the sausage balls and cook for about 5 minutes, until golden, turning regularly with a tongs.

Pile the cavolo nero on top of the sausage balls and cook, stirring frequently, for 2–3 minutes, until completely wilted. Season with salt and pepper, then toss in the toasted pine nuts and half of the Parmesan. Add the drained pasta to the pan, tossing well to combine.

Divide between pasta bowls and scatter the rest of the Parmesan on top to serve.

15 MINS

 15 MINS

 LOADS OF VEG

 FREEZER FRIENDLY

4–6 × 175g (6oz) skinless, boneless haddock fillets

3 tbsp light soy sauce

3 tbsp vegetable stock (from a cube is fine)

1½ tsp sesame oil

1 tsp honey

1 lime, very thinly sliced

1 fresh long red chilli, deseeded and thinly sliced

1 × 5cm (2in) piece of fresh root ginger, peeled and cut into matchsticks

4 spring onions, trimmed and shredded

TO SERVE

boiled jasmine rice

steamed baby pak choi

handful of fresh coriander leaves

Steamed Haddock with Lime, Chilli and Ginger Serves 4–6

This recipe works perfectly with any firm-fleshed fish, such as cod, hake, whiting, coley or even salmon. While the fish is in the oven, cook the jasmine rice and steam the pak choi and you'll have dinner on the table in less than half an hour.

Preheat the oven to 200°C (400°F/gas mark 6).

Place the haddock fillets on two double-thickness squares of foil large enough to make a parcel.

Mix the soy sauce, stock, sesame oil and honey together in a small bowl and drizzle over the fillets. Arrange the limes slices on top, then scatter over the chilli, ginger and spring onions. Close up the parcel loosely and place on a baking tray. Bake in the preheated oven for 10 minutes, then leave to rest, unopened, for another 5 minutes.

Serve the haddock with jasmine rice and steamed pak choi and scatter over the coriander leaves to serve.

CHAPTER 3 CUPBOARD'S BARE

15 MINS

 40 MINS

Risotto with Petit Pois and Smoked Bacon Serves 4-6

2 tbsp rapeseed oil

1 large onion, finely chopped

2 garlic cloves, crushed

100g (4oz) piece of rindless streaky bacon or pancetta, cut into lardons

450g (1lb) Arborio (risotto) rice

about 1.5 litres (2½ pints) chicken or vegetable stock (from a cube is fine)

450g (1lb) frozen petit pois (or just use regular frozen peas, depending on what you have)

50g (2oz) freshly grated Parmesan cheese, plus extra shavings to serve

sea salt and freshly ground black pepper

A risotto is a brilliant store cupboard dinner and who doesn't have a packet of petit pois in the freezer and some bacon in the fridge? Once when I didn't have bacon I used a packet of sausages that I took out of their skins and broke up into small pieces and it was actually really tasty!

Heat the rapeseed oil in a large sauté pan over a medium heat. Add the onion and garlic and cook gently for 3–4 minutes, stirring occasionally, until softened but not coloured. Add the bacon or pancetta and cook for another 2–3 minutes, until crisp and lightly golden. Increase the heat, stir in the rice and cook gently for 1 minute, stirring continuously, until the rice is opaque and fragrant.

Meanwhile, pour the stock into a separate pan and bring to a gentle simmer. Add a ladleful of stock to the rice and cook gently, stirring, until absorbed. Continue to add the simmering stock a ladleful at a time, stirring frequently. Allow each addition of stock to be almost completely absorbed before adding the next ladleful, until the rice is al dente (tender with a slight bite). This should take about 20 minutes.

About 2 minutes before the risotto is ready, stir in the petit pois or peas and allow to finish cooking. Stir in the Parmesan and season to taste with salt and pepper. Leave to rest and swell a little more for 3 minutes. Ladle into warmed shallow bowls and scatter over the Parmesan shavings to serve.

20 MINS

 15 MINS

Gorgonzola Soufflé Omelette with Broad Bean and Rocket Salad Serves 2–4

6 large eggs, separated

1 tsp finely chopped fresh sage (or use a pinch of dried)

15g (½oz) butter

100g (4oz) Gorgonzola cheese, cut into slices and rind removed

sea salt and freshly ground black pepper

FOR THE BROAD BEAN AND ROCKET SALAD

225g (8oz) frozen broad beans

100g (4oz) rocket

1 small red onion, thinly sliced

2 tsp cold pressed rapeseed oil

1 tsp balsamic vinegar

TO SERVE

crusty sourdough bread, to serve (use part-baked bread)

Omelettes are so quick to make and this flavourful version is completely delicious, but if you don't have Gorgonzola to hand, use any soft pungent cheese and a sprinkling of herbs – thyme will work with most.

Cook the broad beans in a pan of boiling salted water over a medium heat for 2–3 minutes or according to the packet instructions. Drain in a colander and rinse under cold water so that they are easier to handle, then slip the broad beans out of their outer skins and discard. Place the rocket in a salad bowl with the red onion and podded broad beans and set aside.

Separate the eggs and put the yolks in a large bowl and the whites in another. Stir the sage into the egg yolks and season with pepper.

Preheat the grill and heat a large non-stick frying pan with a base that's about 25cm (10in) in diameter.

Whisk the egg whites until soft peaks have formed, then fold them into the egg yolk mixture.

Add the butter to the pan and once it has stopped sizzling, quickly add the egg mixture using a spatula. Cook over a low heat for 4–5 minutes.

Toss the rocket salad with the oil and vinegar and season with salt and pepper.

Scatter the Gorgonzola over the omelette, then flash under the grill for 30 seconds. Serve straight to the table with the rocket and broad bean salad and some crusty bread.

15 MINS

 35 MINS

 LOADS OF VEG

 FREEZER FRIENDLY (SOUP)

Instant Tomato Soup with Sourdough Cheese Toasties
Serves 4–6

2 tbsp rapeseed oil

2 large onions, finely chopped

2 garlic cloves, finely chopped

4 × 400g (14oz) tins of Italian chopped tomatoes

good pinch of caster sugar

sea salt and freshly ground black pepper

FOR THE SOURDOUGH CHEESE TOASTIES

100g (4oz) butter

8 slices of sourdough bread (from a large cob loaf)

2 tbsp plain flour

200ml (7fl oz) milk

175g (6oz) Gruyère or mature Cheddar cheese, grated

1 heaped tbsp Dijon mustard

TO GARNISH

snipped fresh chives

This clever soup has a wonderfully intense tomato flavour and doesn't even need stock! It's delicious served with these cheese toasties, which are really like a classic croque monsieur. You can use any cheese that has a good strong flavour and good melting properties.

To make the soup, heat the oil in a large pan over a medium-low heat. Add the onions and garlic and cook for about 10 minutes, stirring occasionally, until softened and lightly golden.

Stir in the tomatoes and sugar and season to taste with salt and pepper. Bring to a simmer and cook gently for 15–20 minutes, stirring occasionally, until the flavours are well combined. Blitz the soup with a hand-held blender until smooth.

Meanwhile, to make the cheese toasties, preheat the grill to medium-hot and melt the butter in a small pan. Brush one side of each slice of bread with some of the melted butter, then toast under the grill, butter side up, for 1–2 minutes, until crisp and golden. Set aside.

Stir the flour into the rest of the butter and cook for 1 minute, then gradually whisk in the milk until smooth. Simmer for a few minutes, until thickened, then take off the heat and stir in one-quarter of the cheese, until melted. Season with salt and pepper.

Spread four of the untoasted sides of the bread with mustard, then top with the rest of the cheese. Grill for a couple of minutes, until the cheese has melted. Top with the rest of the bread, toasted side up, pressing down gently. Put on a foil-lined grill tray and top with the cheese sauce. Grill for about 5 minutes, until bubbling and golden. Slice in half on the diagonal and put on plates.

If you think the soup is too thick, add a little water, then reheat gently. Ladle into soup bowls and garnish with snipped fresh chives, then put on plates with the cheese toasties alongside to serve.

20 MINS

 55 MINS

 LOADS OF VEG

 FREEZER FRIENDLY

1 × 290g (10¼oz) jar of roasted peppers in olive oil

1 onion, finely chopped

1 large carrot, finely chopped

1 celery stick, finely chopped

1 tbsp spicy pepper and herb seasoning (from the Dunnes Stores Simply Better range)

1 heaped tbsp tomato purée

1 tbsp harissa chilli paste

1 × 400g (14oz) tin of Italian chopped tomatoes

350ml (12fl oz) vegetable stock (from a cube is fine)

225g (8oz) red lentils, well rinsed

1 × 400g (14oz) tin of black beans, drained and rinsed

sea salt and freshly ground black pepper

TO GARNISH

lime wedges

4–6 tbsp thick Greek yoghurt

shredded Little Gem lettuce

TO SERVE

corn and wheat tortillas

Red Lentil and Black Bean Chilli with Yoghurt Serves 4-6

This is a very economical dish and is delicious garnished with a dollop of yoghurt. Serve with corn and wheat tortillas that you can now buy in the supermarkets. They are super soft and flexible straight out of the packet and have a long shelf life. To keep it dairy free, add a dollop of hummus instead of the yoghurt.

Drain the oil from the peppers and reserve, then finely chop the peppers. Put 2 tablespoons of the oil in a large deep pan over a medium heat, then add all the vegetables, including the peppers, and sauté for 8–10 minutes, until softened and lightly golden. Sprinkle over the spicy pepper and herb seasoning and stir to combine, then stir in the tomato purée and harissa and cook for another minute.

Stir the in the tomatoes and stock, then add the lentils. Give everything a good stir and cover with a lid. Reduce the heat to low and simmer gently for 30 minutes, until the lentils and vegetables are completely tender.

Stir in the black beans, season with salt and pepper and simmer gently, uncovered, for another 5 minutes.

To serve, ladle the chilli onto plates and garnish with lime wedges, dollops of yoghurt and a mound of shredded lettuce. Serve the tortillas on the side.

15 MINS

 45 MINS

 FREEZER FRIENDLY

4 red onions, thinly sliced

juice of 3 limes

pinch of caster sugar

2 tbsp rapeseed oil

2 carrots, finely chopped

2 celery sticks, finely chopped

4 garlic cloves, crushed

4 tsp ground cumin

1 tsp dried chilli flakes

2 × 400g (14oz) tins of black beans, drained and rinsed

1.2 litres (2 pints) vegetable or chicken stock (from a cube is fine)

sea salt and freshly ground black pepper

TO GARNISH

fresh coriander leaves (optional)

soured cream (optional)

TO SERVE

tortilla chips

Black Bean Soup with Tortilla Chips Serves 4-6

This healthy soup is made in no time with canned beans, some basic aromatics and Cuban-inspired spices. It's incredibly flavourful and delicious and if you want to keep it gluten free, it's worth buying the tortilla chips that are clearly marked as such.

First make the pickled red onions – mix one of the sliced onions with half of the lime juice in a small bowl. Add the sugar and season with salt and pepper. Set aside to pickle for at least 30 minutes. These will keep for up to a week covered in the fridge.

Meanwhile, heat the rapeseed oil in a pan over a medium-high heat. Add the rest of the sliced onions along with the carrots, celery and some salt and pepper. Cook for about 10 minutes, until softened. Stir in the garlic, cumin and chilli flakes and cook for about 30 seconds, until fragrant.

Add the black beans and stock and bring to a simmer. Reduce the heat to a gentle simmer and cook for 30 minutes, until the beans are meltingly tender. Blitz with a hand-held blender to roughly blend – you still want plenty of texture – and season with salt and pepper.

To serve, stir in the rest of the lime juice to taste, then ladle into bowls. Drain the pickled onions, then add to the soup and top with fresh coriander leaves and soured cream (if using). Serve with tortilla chips on the side.

15 MINS

 30 MINS

 LOADS OF VEG

 FREEZER FRIENDLY

Sweetcorn and Chorizo Fritters with Soured Cream and Tomato Country Relish
Serves 4-6

675g (1½lb) frozen sweetcorn kernels (or you can use 2 × 400g (14oz) tins and drain well)

knob of butter

1 onion, finely chopped

4 tbsp cream

vegetable oil, for frying

1 raw chorizo sausage, skinned and diced (approx. 100g (4oz))

2 spring onions, finely chopped

50g (2oz) plain flour

25g (1oz) cornflour

2 tbsp chopped fresh flat-leaf parsley (optional)

1½ tsp baking powder

sea salt and freshly ground black pepper

FOR THE SOURED CREAM DIP

150g (5oz) soured cream

4 tbsp thick Greek yoghurt

2 tbsp snipped fresh chives, plus extra to garnish (optional)

1 tsp Dijon mustard

TO SERVE

tomato country relish

lightly dressed mixed salad

This is a great one to have up your sleeve, as nearly everything you need for the fritters is a store cupboard ingredient. If you don't have any chorizo, try using some leftover diced ham or crispy pancetta.

If using frozen sweetcorn, cook in a pan of boiling water with a pinch of salt for 3–4 minutes or according to the packet instructions. Drain well.

Melt the butter in a saucepan over a medium heat, add the onion and sauté for 8–10 minutes, until softened. Stir in half of the sweetcorn and season to taste. Stir in the cream and blitz with a hand-held blender until you have achieved a rough purée.

Heat a large non-stick frying pan over a medium-high heat and add a little oil. Tip in the chorizo and sauté for 2–3 minutes, until sizzling. Drain on kitchen paper.

Mix the creamed sweetcorn in a bowl with the reserved whole kernels, spring onions, plain flour, cornflour, parsley (if using), baking powder and plenty of seasoning, then fold in the chorizo.

Wipe out the frying pan and reheat with enough oil to shallow fry. Working in batches, add large spoonfuls of the mixture into the pan and cook for 2–3 minutes on each side, until crisp and golden brown. Keep warm in a low oven.

Meanwhile, mix the soured cream with the yoghurt, chives (if using), mustard and plenty of freshly ground black pepper. Place in a serving bowl.

Drain the fritters briefly on kitchen paper, then arrange on a large serving platter or individual plates with the soured cream dip and a separate bowl of the tomato country relish. Scatter over the chives (if using) to serve. A nice big bowl of mixed salad will balance the meal perfectly.

20 MINS

 50 MINS

 LOADS OF VEG

2 litres (3½ pints) chicken or vegetable stock (from a cube is fine)

2 tbsp rapeseed oil

50g (2oz) butter, diced

1 small onion, finely chopped

1 garlic clove, finely chopped

1 tsp fresh thyme leaves, plus extra to garnish

675g (1½lb) any root vegetable or use a mixture, such as carrots, parsnips and celeriac, peeled and diced (see the note in the intro)

450g (1lb) Arborio (risotto) rice

150ml (¼ pint) dry white wine

5 tbsp freshly grated Parmesan cheese, plus extra to garnish

sea salt and freshly ground black pepper

Throw-It-All-In Root Vegetable Risotto
Serves 4-6

Risottos are just brilliant, as they are a wonderful blank canvas to enhance with what you have in the fridge. Any root vegetable on its own works well, as does a mixture, as all their flavours have an affinity with each other.

Pour the stock into a pan and bring up to a gentle simmer.

Heat the oil and half of the butter in a separate large pan. Add the onion, garlic and thyme and cook over a medium heat for 2–3 minutes, stirring occasionally, until softened but not coloured.

Stir in the root vegetables and cook for another 6–8 minutes, until the vegetables are almost but not quite cooked through and just beginning to pick up a bit of colour.

Increase the heat, then add the rice and cook for 1 minute, stirring continuously, until all the grains are evenly coated and the rice is opaque. Pour in the wine and allow it to reduce for 1–2 minutes, stirring.

Reduce the heat to medium, then add a ladleful of stock, stirring until it is completely absorbed. Continue to add the simmering stock a ladleful at a time, stirring frequently. Allow each addition of stock to be almost completely absorbed before adding the next ladleful, until the rice is al dente (just tender but with a slight bite). This should take about 20 minutes and you might have a little stock left, depending on the rice you use.

Just before serving, stir in the remaining butter along with the Parmesan and season to taste. Ladle the risotto into warmed bowls and garnish with the extra Parmesan cheese and thyme leaves to serve.

15 MINS

 20 MINS

 LOADS OF VEG

 FREEZER FRIENDLY

2 tbsp rapeseed oil

2 shallots, finely chopped

100g (4oz) smoked bacon or pancetta, diced

450g (1lb) frozen peas

6 fresh mint leaves, plus extra to garnish

900ml (1½ pints) chicken or vegetable stock (from a cube is fine)

4–6 tbsp soured cream

sea salt and freshly ground black pepper

TO SERVE

ciabatta bread (use part-baked rolls) (optional)

Pea and Mint Soup with Smoked Bacon Serves 4–6

This soup has to be as instant as you are ever going to get. It literally takes minutes to prepare and is good served either hot or cold. If you fancy a healthier version, omit the soured cream and just garnish with a good grinding of black pepper.

Heat the oil in a pan over a medium heat. Add the shallots and sauté for 2–3 minutes, stirring occasionally, until softened but not coloured.

Add the smoked bacon or pancetta and continue to sauté for another 3–4 minutes, until sizzling and lightly golden.

Add the peas (reserving a few to garnish) and mint and stir until well coated, then pour in the stock and bring to the boil. Season to taste with salt and pepper, then reduce the heat to a simmer and cook for 3 minutes, stirring, to allow the flavours to combine.

Pour the soup into a food processor and blend until smooth, then pour back into the pan (or use a hand-held blender). Season to taste and reheat gently.

Ladle the soup into warmed bowls. Swirl in the soured cream and add a good grinding of black pepper. Garnish with the reserved peas and the fresh mint leaves and arrange some ciabatta bread alongside, if liked, to serve.

10 MINS

 30 MINS

Saffron Orzo with Smoked Salmon and Peas Serves 4–6

2 large pinches of saffron threads or 1 tsp ground turmeric

350g (12oz) orzo pasta

225ml (8fl oz) cream

finely grated rind of 1 lemon

225g (8oz) frozen peas

2 × 200g (7oz) packets of smoked salmon

sea salt and freshly ground black pepper

TO GARNISH

handful of fresh basil leaves (optional)

This is an element of a dish that I often serve in the restaurant. The orzo pasta takes on a wonderful yellow colour from the saffron, and although it is a dish that raids the fridge or freezer, it's nice enough to serve for a kitchen supper when you've got friends over. The smoked salmon could also be replaced with hot smoked salmon or trout or even cooked ham.

Bring a large pan of salted water to the boil with the saffron or turmeric. Tip in the orzo pasta, stir once and cook for 10–12 minutes, until just al dente (tender but firm to the bite), or according to the packet instructions. Reserve a small cup of the cooking water, then drain the pasta well and rinse under cold running water.

Place the cream in a large pan with the lemon rind. Bring to the boil, then reduce the heat and simmer for 2 minutes. Add the cooked orzo and the peas and simmer for another 1–2 minutes, stirring occasionally. Season to taste with salt and pepper, then tear in the smoked salmon and add enough of the reserved pasta cooking water to make a silky-smooth sauce. Divide between plates and scatter over the basil (if using) to serve.

30 MINS

 1 HR 15 MINS

 LOADS OF VEG

 FREEZER FRIENDLY

1 large butternut squash (or small pumpkin) or cauliflower or 500g (1lb 2oz) frozen spinach

rapeseed oil, optional (if roasting the veg)

100g (4oz) butter

1 onion, finely chopped

2 celery sticks, finely chopped

100g (4oz) plain flour

1 litre (1¾ pints) milk

1 tbsp prepared English mustard

200g (7oz) Cheddar cheese, grated

500g (1lb 2oz) macaroni pasta

sea salt and freshly ground black pepper

TO SERVE

roasted cherry tomatoes on the vine (optional)

Super Loaded Mac 'n' Cheese
Serves 4–6

A brilliant recipe for getting lots of nutritional goodness into an unsuspecting crowd! It can easily be scaled up to feed large numbers very economically and would be delicious served with a green salad or roasted cherry tomatoes on the vine.

If using butternut squash or pumpkin, peel it and remove the seeds, then cut into even-sized pieces. If using cauliflower, break it into florets. Steam for 10–12 minutes, until tender. (Alternatively, you could cut the squash or pumpkin into large wedges, leave the cauliflower as florets and drizzle with a little rapeseed oil and roast in the oven at 200°C (400°F/gas mark 6) for about 40 minutes, until tender.) If using spinach, cook it according to the packet instructions. Tip your veg into a food processor and blend to a smooth purée (or mash to a rough purée with a potato masher).

Preheat the oven to 180°C (350°F/gas mark 4).

Melt the butter in a pan over a medium to low heat. Add the onion and celery and sauté for 2–3 minutes, until softened but not coloured. Stir in the flour and cook for 1 minute, stirring with a wooden spoon. Gradually pour in the milk, whisking until smooth after each addition. Season with salt and pepper. Bring to the boil, then reduce the heat and simmer gently for 2–3 minutes, stirring occasionally, until smooth and thickened. Blitz with a hand-held blender until smooth, then stir in the mustard and most of the cheese. Remove from the heat.

Bring the macaroni to the boil in a large pan of boiling water with a pinch of salt, then reduce the heat and cook for 7 minutes – it should not be completely cooked at this point. Drain in a colander and return to the pan. Fold in the cheese sauce along with the vegetable purée.

Transfer to a large ovenproof dish and scatter over the remaining cheese, then bake in the preheated oven for 30 minutes, until bubbling and lightly golden. Serve straight to the table with roasted cherry tomatoes on the vine, if liked.

20 MINS

 1 HR

 LOADS OF VEG

Shakshuka (Middle Eastern Baked Eggs) Serves 4–6

1 × 290g (10¼oz) jar of roasted peppers in olive oil

1 large onion, thinly sliced

4 garlic cloves, crushed

2 tsp sweet paprika

½ tsp cumin seeds

½–1 tsp cayenne pepper (to taste)

2 × 400g (14oz) tins of whole cherry tomatoes

1 tbsp lemon juice

2 tsp caster sugar

4–8 eggs (depending on how hungry you are)

sea salt and freshly ground black pepper

TO GARNISH

fresh coriander leaves (optional)

crumbled feta cheese

sizzling chorizo sausage

Greek yoghurt (optional)

TO SERVE

chargrilled sourdough bread

This Tunisian-inspired recipe of baked eggs on a bed of spiced peppers and tomatoes is a great dish for when there's nothing much in the fridge. Choose the final embellishments depending on what you have.

Drain the olive oil from the peppers into a sauté pan over a medium heat. Dice the peppers and set aside until needed.

Add the onion to the hot oil and sauté for about 5 minutes, until it has just started to pick up some colour. Stir in the garlic and spices and cook for another few minutes.

Pour in the tomatoes and roughly mash. Stir in the reserved peppers along with the lemon juice and sugar and bring to the boil, then turn down the heat and simmer for 30 minutes. Season with salt and pepper.

Make four to eight holes in the pepper mix using the back of a wooden spoon just large enough to fit the eggs, then crack one egg into each hole. Season them lightly, turn the heat down as low as possible, cover the pan and cook for 8–10 minutes, until the eggs are just set.

Scatter over the coriander (if using), feta and chorizo and serve straight to the table with plenty of chargrilled sourdough bread to mop up all the delicious juices. If serving with Greek yoghurt, put a separate bowl on the table so that everyone can help themselves.

20 MINS

 35 MINS

 LOADS OF VEG

Fusilli Lunghi with Ham, Broad Beans, Leeks and Croutons
Serves 4–6

4 tbsp rapeseed oil

1 ciabatta loaf, cut or torn into small pieces (a stale or part-baked loaf is perfect)

2 garlic cloves, finely chopped

½ tsp dried chilli flakes

550g (1¼lb) leeks, trimmed and sliced

500g (1lb 2oz) Dunnes Stores Simply Better Bronze Die Fusilli Lunghi (or you can use linguine or spaghetti)

300g (11oz) frozen broad beans

2 × 120g (4½oz) packets of cooked ham chunks, chopped

sea salt and freshly ground black pepper

Broad beans are an excellent ingredient to have tucked away in the freezer. Once you have slipped off their outer silver skins, they have the most wonderful vibrant green colour and make a nice change from peas if you've not got much in.

Heat half of the oil in a large frying pan over a medium heat. Add the ciabatta cubes and toss them in the hot oil for 4–5 minutes, until golden. Sprinkle over the garlic and chilli flakes, season with salt and pepper and toss for another 30 seconds or so, until fragrant. Tip into a bowl and set aside until needed.

Wipe out the frying pan, add the rest of the oil and set the pan over a medium heat. Add the leeks and cook for 8–10 minutes, until meltingly tender. Season to taste with salt and pepper.

Meanwhile, cook the pasta in a large pan of boiling salted water for 10–12 minutes, until al dente (just tender to the bite), or according to the packet instructions.

Cook the broad beans in a pan of boiling salted water over a medium heat for 2–3 minutes or according to the packet instructions. Drain in a colander and rinse under cold water so that they are easier to handle, then slip the broad beans out of their outer skins and discard.

Drain the pasta, reserving 2 tablespoons of the cooking water, then return it to the pan along with the reserved cooking water. Fold in the leeks, podded broad beans and the ham and place back on the heat for 1–2 minutes, stirring, to allow everything to warm through. Finally, fold in the ciabatta croutons and gently toss together to combine. Serve in pasta bowls and add a good grinding of black pepper.

20 MINS

 1 HR

 LOADS OF VEG

❄ FREEZER FRIENDLY

1kg (2¼lb) small pumpkin (such as Crown Prince – see the intro), peeled, seeded and chopped

4 raw chorizo sausages, cases removed and torn into pieces

1 tbsp rapeseed oil

250g (9oz) frozen spinach, thawed and squeezed dry

150g (5oz) soft rindless goat's cheese, crumbled

100g (4oz) shop-bought red onion relish

8 large eggs

250ml (9fl oz) cream

sea salt and freshly ground black pepper

TO SERVE

slices of chargrilled sourdough bread (optional)

Pumpkin, Chorizo and Spinach Frittata Serves 6–8

Pumpkins will keep for many months if correctly stored. They don't like too much heat or the bitter cold, so the bottom shelf of a well-ventilated store cupboard is perfect. A small one is the right size for this recipe. Look out for the delicious blue-skinned Crown Prince, which has a wonderful flavour. Otherwise there are a number of small orange-coloured varieties readily available in farmers markets and most Asian supermarkets. Otherwise use butternut squash.

Preheat the oven to 220°C (425°F/gas mark 7).

Place the pumpkin and chorizo in a 30cm (12in) deep ovenproof frying pan or similar-sized baking dish. Drizzle with the oil and season with salt and pepper. Roast in the preheated oven for 15 minutes, until the pumpkin is lightly golden and just tender. Remove from the oven.

Reduce the oven temperature to 200°C (400°F/gas mark 6).

Add the spinach, goat's cheese and red onion relish to the pan and gently fold everything together.

Break the eggs into a bowl and add the cream, then season with salt and pepper. Using a fork, whisk gently to combine, then pour over the vegetable and cheese mixture in the pan.

Bake in the oven for 25–30 minutes, until puffed up and golden. Remove from the oven and leave to cool a little, then cut into slices and serve on plates with slices of chargrilled sourdough bread, if liked.

15 MINS

 15 MINS

 LOADS OF VEG

500g (1lb 2oz) spaghetti

1 tbsp rapeseed oil

1 large red onion, thinly sliced

4 garlic cloves, sliced

6 anchovy fillets from a jar or tin, drained and finely chopped

1 × 400g (14oz) tin of Italian chopped tomatoes

1 × 290g (10¼oz) jar of roasted peppers in oilve oil, well drained and thinly sliced

1 × 200g (7oz) carton or jar of black olives, pitted

225g (8oz) frozen spinach

2 heaped tbsp rinsed capers

sea salt and freshly ground black pepper

Spaghetti Puttanesca with Spinach Serves 4–6

Using frozen spinach is a great way to access a green vegetable when the cupboard is bare and the flavours work really well in this Italian classic. Frozen spinach comes in cubes, so it's super easy to use, which is why I always have a bag tucked away. It's also less watery then the fresh variety, so it doesn't thin out the sauce – a win-win!

Cook the pasta according to the packet instructions.

Meanwhile, heat the oil in a large frying pan over a medium heat. Add the onion and sauté for 6–8 minutes, until softened and just beginning to catch around the edges. Add the garlic and anchovies and cook for another minute.

Add the tomatoes, peppers, olives, spinach and capers to the pan. Season lightly with salt, as the anchovies are already salty, and plenty of black pepper and cook for 2–3 minutes, until the spinach has defrosted and is nicely incorporated into the sauce.

Drain the pasta into a colander in the sink, then toss into the sauce until evenly combined. Divide between pasta bowls to serve.

15 MINS

 15 MINS

 LOADS OF VEG

Artichoke, Broad Bean and Pea Tartines Serves 2–4

1 × 290g (10¼oz) jar of grilled artichokes in olive oil

2 onions, sliced

4 garlic cloves, thinly sliced

150g (5oz) frozen peas

150g (5oz) frozen broad beans

finely grated rind of 1 small lemon

good pinch of dried chilli flakes

4 thick slices of sourdough bread (fresh or frozen)

100g (4oz) thinly sliced prosciutto

sea salt and freshly ground black pepper

I came up with this recipe one day after a rummage around the kitchen for something tasty to eat. The prosciutto is arranged on thick slices of sourdough (which freezes brilliantly once it has been sliced), then piled high with the vegetables – what's not to love?

Drain the oil from the artichokes into a sauté pan over a medium heat. Add the onions and cook for 3–4 minutes, until translucent. Season with salt and pepper, then add the garlic and cook for another 3–4 minutes, until well softened.

Add the artichokes, peas, broad beans, lemon rind and chilli. Cook for 2–3 minutes, until all the flavours have mingled together.

Meanwhile, chargrill or toast the sourdough bread and arrange on plates. Add a layer of prosciutto, then pile the vegetable mixture on top to serve.

15 MINS

 20 MINS

 LOADS OF VEG

50g (2oz) pine nuts

4 tbsp rapeseed oil

20g (¾oz) fresh sage, leaves stripped (optional)

175g (6oz) pancetta or smoked streaky bacon lardons

1kg (2¼lb) small pumpkin, peeled, seeded and cut into small pieces

2 × 250g (9oz) packets of buffalo milk ricotta and spinach ravioli

50g (2oz) freshly grated Parmesan cheese, plus extra to serve

drizzle of good-quality balsamic vinegar

sea salt and freshly ground black pepper

Ravioli with Pumpkin, Pancetta and Pine Nuts Serves 4–6

Look out for small organic pumpkins, which are normally a bright, vibrant orange, as their size is perfect for this recipe. Once the pumpkin is peeled and seeded you should end up with just over 450g (1lb) of diced flesh. Otherwise a butternut squash is an excellent alternative and both keep for months in the bottom of a cool store cupboard.

Preheat the oven to 180°C (350°F/gas mark 4).

Place the pine nuts in a baking tin and roast in the preheated oven for about 3 minutes, until nicely toasted. Remove from the oven and leave to cool.

Heat the oil in a heavy-based pan over a medium-high heat. Add the sage leaves (if using) and fry for 20–30 seconds, until crisp, then lift out and set aside to drain on kitchen paper. Add the pancetta or smoked streaky bacon lardons to the pan and cook for 2–3 minutes, stirring occasionally, until the pancetta or bacon begins to crisp.

Add the pumpkin to the pan and mix well to combine. Season to taste with salt and pepper and cook for 4–5 minutes, stirring occasionally, until the pumpkin is cooked through but still holding its shape, adding a splash of water if you think it needs it.

Bring a large pan of salted water to the boil. Add the ravioli, give it a good stir and cook for 3–4 minutes, until just tender, or according to the packet instructions.

Drain the pasta and add to the pan with the pancetta and pumpkin. Stir in the Parmesan and season to taste with salt and pepper.

Divide between warmed pasta bowls and finish each one with a sprinkling of grated Parmesan, the toasted pine nuts and fried sage leaves (if using), then drizzle with a little balsamic vinegar and add a good grinding of black pepper to serve.

10 MINS

 20 MINS

Glazed Gammon Steaks with Butter Bean and Cheddar Mash
Serves 4-6

1 tbsp rapeseed oil

4-6 × 150g (5oz) gammon steaks (preferably dry cure, such as O'Neill's)

1 tbsp Highbank Organic Orchard Syrup (or use any organic apple syrup)

225g (8oz) frozen soy beans

knob of butter

sea salt and freshly ground black pepper

FOR THE BUTTER BEAN AND CHEDDAR MASH

2 tbsp rapeseed oil

1 small onion, finely chopped

2 garlic cloves, finely chopped

2 fresh rosemary sprigs

2 × 400g (14oz) tins of butter beans, drained and rinsed

4 tbsp milk

100g (4oz) mature Cheddar cheese, grated

Butter bean mash is a fantastic mashed potato alternative that comes together in less than 10 minutes. You can mash it roughly with a potato masher to retain some texture or purée it until it becomes silky smooth. The addition of the Cheddar isn't essential but it adds an extra richness that pairs perfectly with the gammon steaks.

Preheat a large frying pan over a medium heat. Add the oil, then add the gammon steaks and fry for 3 minutes on each side. Add the apple syrup and toss until evenly coated. Season with pepper.

Meanwhile, to make the mash, heat the oil in a pan over a medium heat. Add the onion and sauté for 2–3 minutes, until softened. Add the garlic and rosemary and cook for another minute, until just fragrant. Stir in the butter beans and milk and simmer for 5 minutes, until the beans are heated through. Season with salt and pepper.

Cook the soy beans in a pan of boiling salted water for 4–5 minutes, until tender, then drain and toss in the butter.

Remove the rosemary from the butter bean mixture, then add the Cheddar. Blitz until smooth and creamy in a food processor or using a hand-held blender. Keep warm.

Arrange the butter bean mash on warmed plates, put the gammon steaks on top and drizzle over the juices from the pan. Scatter over the soy beans to serve.

15 MINS

 35 MINS

 FREEZER FRIENDLY

2 × 111g (4½oz) tins of tuna in olive oil, drained (preferably Shines Wild Irish Tuna)

550g (1¼lb) potatoes, cut into small chunks

½ lemon, pips removed

1 heaped tbsp snipped fresh chives

1 egg, beaten

plain flour, for dusting

225g (8oz) frozen spinach

175g (6oz) frozen petit pois

knob of butter

sea salt and freshly ground black pepper

TO SERVE

thick Greek yoghurt swirled with sweet chilli sauce

Tuna Fishcakes with Spinach and Petit Pois Makes 8

Shines Wild Irish Tuna is one of my go-to ingredients when I want to have something healthy and tasty on the table and the cupboards are pretty bare. Connor and Lucia love these fishcakes with a small pot of yoghurt topped with a drizzle of ketchup or sweet chilli sauce.

Open the tins of tuna, drain off the excess olive oil and reserve for frying the fishcakes.

Place the potatoes in a pan, cover with cold salted water and bring to the boil over a medium heat. Once boiling, reduce the heat to a simmer and cook for about 8 minutes, until tender. Drain and leave them to steam dry for 2–3 minutes.

Mash the potatoes, then add the tuna, breaking it up with a fork. Squeeze in the lemon juice to taste, stir in the chives and season with salt and pepper. Add the beaten egg, then use your hands to bring everything together. Divide the mixture into eight even-sized balls and shape into fishcakes. Chill for at least 15 minutes or up to 24 hours is perfect.

Heat the reserved drained olive oil in a large non-stick frying pan over a medium heat. Dust the chilled fishcakes lightly in flour, shaking off any excess, then add to the hot oil and cook for 3–4 minutes on each side, until golden brown.

Meanwhile, cook the spinach and petit pois in a pan of boiling salted water for 2–3 minutes, until just tender. Drain and return to the pan with the butter, tossing to combine.

Arrange the fishcakes on plates with the spinach and petit pois. Add small pots of Greek yoghurt swirled with sweet chilli sauce to serve.

15 MINS

 40 MINS

 LOADS OF VEG

Smoky Sweetcorn Oven-Baked Risotto with Artichokes
Serves 4–6

1 × 290g (10¼oz) jar of grilled artichokes in olive oil

2 chorizo sausages, peeled and diced (about 175g (6oz) in total)

1 large onion, finely chopped

2 celery sticks, finely chopped

good pinch of dried chilli flakes

500g (1lb 2oz) Arborio (risotto) rice

120ml (4fl oz) dry white wine

1 litre (1¾ pints) hot chicken or vegetable stock (from a cube is fine)

225g (8oz) frozen sweetcorn

50g (2oz) freshly grated Parmesan cheese

sea salt and freshly ground black pepper

A jar of grilled artichokes is a brilliant store cupboard stand-by, as they're full of flavour and even come with the oil that you need for a dish. Any remaining oil can be used at a later date. I add them to pasta dishes, stews and risottos or even as a simple bruschetta topping.

Preheat the oven to 200°C (400°F/gas mark 6).

Drain the oil from the jar of artichokes and reserve, then place the artichoke pieces on kitchen paper to remove any excess oil. Set aside until needed.

Add 1 tablespoon of the reserved oil to a deep-sided ovenproof frying pan or casserole over a medium heat. Add the chorizo and sauté for 2–3 minutes, until well rendered and sizzling. Stir in the onion, celery and chilli flakes and cook for another 2–3 minutes, until soft.

Tip the rice into the pan, stirring to coat, and cook for 1 minute. Pour over the wine and allow to bubble down for a few minutes, until absorbed. Pour in the hot stock, then gently fold in the artichokes and sweetcorn. Season to taste with salt and pepper.

Cover with a tight-fitting lid and bake in the preheated oven for 22 minutes, until the rice is almost completely cooked through. Stir in most of the Parmesan and leave to swell for 3 minutes.

Ladle into bowls and scatter over the rest of the Parmesan to serve.

15 MINS

 40 MINS

 LOADS OF VEG

 FREEZER FRIENDLY

600g (1lb 5oz) green lentils

2 tsp ground ginger

2 tsp ground turmeric

1.2 litres (2 pints) water

1 × 400ml (14fl oz) tin of coconut milk

3 tbsp rapeseed oil

4 tsp black mustard seeds

2 tsp dried chilli flakes

1 tsp ground cumin

1 tsp ground coriander

900g (2lb) sweet potatoes, peeled and sliced into half-moons

1 × 400g (14oz) tin of Italian chopped tomatoes

300g (11oz) frozen spinach

juice of 2 lemons

sea salt and freshly ground black pepper

TO GARNISH

fresh coriander leaves (optional)

TO SERVE

warmed small wraps

Green Lentil and Sweet Potato Dhal Serves 4–6

We always have a packet of wraps tucked away in the freezer. I cook them directly on the gas flame to get them lightly charred and nice and fluffy, but you can do them under the grill or in the oven if you prefer.

Put the lentils into a large heavy-based pan with the ginger, 1 teaspoon of the turmeric and 2 teaspoons of salt, then pour over the water and coconut milk. Bring to a gentle simmer and cook for 30 minutes, then whisk really hard until the mixture becomes smooth. If it's too thick, you can add a little more water. Leave gently bubbling while you get your spices ready.

Heat the oil in a small heavy-based frying pan over a low heat. Add the remaining teaspoon of turmeric along with the mustard seeds, chilli flakes, cumin and coriander and leave them to temper. The oil should be bubbling and the seeds should be popping – this will take about 30 seconds to 1 minute. Reduce the heat to very low, add the sweet potatoes and cook for 5–7 minutes, until just tender.

Stir the sweet potato mixture straight into the lentils. The mixture will spit a bit, but that's okay. Whisk again before stirring in the tomatoes, spinach and lemon juice. Season with salt and pepper.

Ladle into warmed bowls, garnish with fresh coriander leaves (if using) and serve the warmed wraps on the side.

15 MINS

 1 HR

LOADS OF VEG

Pearl Barley Risotto with Bacon and Cabbage Serves 4-6

1 tbsp rapeseed oil

15g (½oz) butter

1 onion, diced

4 large carrots, diced

2 leeks, trimmed and sliced

2 celery sticks, diced

2 garlic cloves, finely chopped

1 tsp dried thyme

400g (14oz) pearl barley

1.5 litres (2½ pints) hot chicken stock (from a cube is fine)

1 heaped tbsp Dijon mustard, plus extra to serve

1 Savoy cabbage, cored and shredded

200g (7oz) cooked lean bacon joint or ham, chopped into small pieces

sea salt and freshly ground black pepper

This dish uses pearl barley instead of rice for an interesting nutty texture. It's much cheaper than traditional risotto rice and has the added bonus of being extremely good for you too. I've used a leftover bacon joint here, but you could also use a couple packets of ham chunks.

Heat a large pan over a medium heat. Add the oil and butter, then add the onion, carrots, leeks and celery and sauté for 6–8 minutes, until softened. Stir in the garlic and thyme and cook for another 2–3 minutes, until fragrant.

Stir in the pearl barely and cook for 1 minute, until well combined. Pour in the hot stock, add the mustard and season to taste with a little salt and plenty of pepper. Bring to a simmer, then reduce the heat to low and cook for 35 minutes, stirring occasionally.

Add the cabbage and the bacon or ham and cook for another 5 minutes, until the cabbage is wilted and tender and the bacon is nicely warmed through.

Divide between plates and serve with a dollop of mustard on the side if liked.

10 MINS

 20 MINS

 FREEZER FRIENDLY

4 cubes of frozen spinach (about 175g (6oz))

4 mini ready-made pizza bases (such as Pizza da Piero or use small white or wholemeal wraps)

100g (4oz) passata (from a jar or carton)

4 eggs

125g (4½oz) fresh goat's cheese

50g (2oz) small green or black olives (from a jar or carton)

cold pressed rapeseed oil, for drizzling

4 slices of Parma ham, torn

sea salt and freshly ground black pepper

TO SERVE

lightly dressed baby leaf salad (optional)

Fiorentina Pizzas with Parma Ham Makes 4 mini pizzas

I love supporting an Irish brand and Pizza da Piero is an excellent example. Look out for them in the supermarket chilled section or use the Middle Eastern-style wraps that can puff up, which come in white and wholemeal varieties.

Preheat the oven to 200°C (400°F/gas mark 6).

Place the spinach in a pan over a high heat and pour over enough boiling water to cover. Bring to a simmer and cook for 1–2 minutes, until just defrosted. Drain into a colander and leave to cool a little, then squeeze out any excess moisture.

Place the mini ready-made pizza bases or wraps on a large baking sheet. Spread with the passata and arrange small mounds of spinach on top. Break an egg into the centre of each one, then crumble over the goat's cheese and scatter the olives on top. Drizzle each one with a little oil, then bake in the preheated oven for 6–8 minutes, until piping hot and golden. Arrange the pizzas on plates and add the torn Parma ham just before serving with some baby leaf salad on the side if liked.

20 MINS

 30 MINS

 LOADS OF VEG

Lentil and Tomato Salad with Paneer and Poppadums
Serves 4-6

350g (12oz) Puy lentils

1.2 litres (2 pints) water

juice of 1 small lemon

juice of 1 small lime

1 tbsp white wine vinegar

2 red onions, thinly sliced into rings

4 tbsp rapeseed oil

250g (9oz) paneer, well drained and cut into cubes

1 garlic clove, crushed

4 tbsp spiced mango chutney, plus extra to garnish

2 tsp garam masala

300g (11oz) cherry tomatoes on the vine, halved (or use semi sun-dried tomatoes instead if you've no fresh to hand)

200g (7oz) baby spinach

20g (¾oz) fresh coriander, leaves stripped and roughly chopped, but some whole leaves reserved for garnish

sea salt and freshly ground black pepper

TO SERVE

poppadums

shop-bought tzatziki

This Indian-inspired salad uses paneer, which is very popular in Indian dishes. It's now available in our larger supermarkets and looks similar to feta, but it isn't as salty. It doesn't melt so it holds its shape well, plus it has a decent shelf life, so it's well worth keeping a packet handy in the fridge.

Rinse the lentils in a sieve under cold running water, then place in a pan with the water. Add a pinch of salt and bring to the boil, then reduce the heat and simmer for 15–20 minutes, until al dente (tender but still with a little bite).

Meanwhile, place the lemon and lime juice and the vinegar in a large bowl with a good pinch of salt. Toss in the onion rings and after a few minutes they will turn pink.

Heat 1 tablespoon of the oil in a frying pan over a medium heat. Add the paneer and sauté for about 5 minutes, turning regularly, until golden.

To make the dressing, whisk the rest of the oil in a small bowl with the garlic, mango chutney and garam masala. Fold into the paneer, tossing to coat and glaze.

Drain the lentils and add to the onion rings, tossing to combine. Fold in the dressed paneer along with the tomatoes, spinach and coriander.

Divide between plates and garnish with the fresh coriander leaves. Serve with poppadums, tzatziki and extra mango chutney.

15 MINS

 30 MINS

 LOADS OV VEG

❄ FREEZER FRIENDLY (RAGÙ)

1 × 290g (10¼oz) jar of roasted peppers in olive oil

1 onion, finely chopped

1 large carrot, finely chopped

1 celery stick, finely chopped

12 pork sausages (about 650g (1lb 7oz) – I used Jane Russell's toasted fennel and chilli sausages)

1 × 400g (14oz) tin of Italian chopped tomatoes

1 heaped tbsp tomato purée

200ml (7fl oz) chicken stock (from a cube is fine)

200g (7oz) instant polenta

100g (4oz) mature Cheddar cheese, finely grated

knob of butter

sea salt and freshly ground black pepper

Cheesy Polenta with Sausage Ragù Serves 4-6

Instant polenta is made by grinding corn into meal and takes just a few minutes to make, as it comes part cooked. It's very bland, so it needs to be seasoned correctly and enriched with cheese and a little butter, then it can taste very nice indeed!

Drain the oil off the jar of peppers and add it to a large heavy-based casserole over a medium to high heat. Add the onion, carrot and celery and cook for about 5 minutes, until well softened and beginning to pick up a bit of colour. Stir in the sausages, breaking them up into small pieces as you go, and cook for another 6–8 minutes, until the sausages are nicely browned.

Meanwhile, finely chop the roasted peppers. Add them to the sausage mixture along with the tomatoes, tomato purée and stock. Bring to a simmer, then reduce the heat and cook for 8–10 minutes, until the sauce is well reduced and thickened. Season with salt and pepper.

While the ragù is bubbling away, make the polenta by following the packet instructions. Remove from the heat and stir in most of the cheese along with the butter and season with salt and pepper to taste.

Divide the polenta between warmed plates and top with the sausage ragù. Add the rest of the cheese to serve.

15 MINS

 40 MINS

Mediterranean Tuna, Pepper and Artichoke Tart
Serves 4-6

1 × 640g (1lb 6oz) packet of frozen ready-rolled puff pastry, thawed at room temperature for 2 hours

1 egg, beaten with a pinch of salt

1 × 290g (10¼oz) jar of grilled artichokes in olive oil

1 × 290g (10¼oz) jar of roasted peppers in olive oil

2 × 150g (5oz) packets of garlic and herb soft cheese (such as Boursin)

2 × 111g (4¼oz) tins of tuna in olive oil, drained (such as Shines Wild Irish Tuna)

2 tbsp capers, well rinsed

1 × 100g (4oz) carton or jar of pitted black olives

TO GARNISH

shop-bought basil pesto

TO SERVE

lightly dressed fresh green salad

Any cream cheese will work for this recipe, but one with some garlic and herbs already added is particularly nice. Cream cheese is a great thing to have tucked away in the back of the fridge and has a decent shelf life, which makes it the perfect ingredient for this colourful tart.

Preheat the oven to 220°C (425°F/gas mark 7). Line two large baking sheets with non-stick baking paper.

Unroll the two pastry sheets onto the two lined baking sheets. Score a 1cm (½in) border around the edges with a sharp knife, taking care not to cut through the pastry. Prick the area inside the border all over with a fork. Brush with the beaten egg, then bake in the preheated oven for 15 minutes. Remove from the oven and leave to cool a little.

Meanwhile, drain the oil off the artichokes and peppers and reserve to use in other dishes. Cut the artichokes into thin wedges and cut the peppers into strips. Drain both on kitchen paper to remove any excess oil.

Spread each tart with one packet of the garlic and herb soft cheese, then arrange the peppers over it. Add the artichokes, then scatter over the tuna and capers and dot with the olives. Bake in the oven for another 15 minutes (swapping the shelves so that whichever one you cooked on the top first is on the bottom) until the pastry is golden, puffed up and cooked through. Drizzle over the pesto to garnish.

Cut into slices and serve on plates with some green salad, if liked.

CHAPTER 4 SLOW AND LOW

15 MINS

 4¼ HRS

 LOADS OF VEG

 FREEZER FRIENDLY

3 tbsp rapeseed oil

2 aubergines, trimmed and cut into 5cm (2in) batons

1 large onion, finely chopped

4 garlic cloves, crushed

1 × 5cm (2in) piece of fresh root ginger, peeled and finely grated

1 tbsp ground cumin

2 tsp ground coriander

2 tsp garam masala

1 tsp cayenne pepper

2 × 400g (14oz) tins of chickpeas, drained and rinsed

1 × 400g (14oz) tin of Italian chopped tomatoes

300ml (½ pint) vegetable stock (from a cube is fine)

250ml (9fl oz) coconut cream

sea salt and freshly ground black pepper

TO GARNISH

roughly chopped fresh coriander

TO SERVE

poppadums

mango chutney

shop-bought tzatziki

Aubergine and Chickpea Rogan Josh Serves 4–6

I'm using canned chickpeas in this recipe, as although dried chickpeas can cook beautifully in the slow cooker, by the time they're done the aubergine would have lost all of its wonderful silky texture.

Preheat your slow cooker according to the manufacturer's instructions. If your slow cooker has a sauté option, you can use this; if not, use a large sauté pan on the hob over a medium-high heat. Add the oil, then add the aubergines and sauté for 8–10 minutes, until lightly golden but still firm. Stir in the onion, garlic and ginger and cook for another 2–3 minutes, until evenly combined and the onion has started to soften. Stir in the spices and cook for another minute or so, until fragrant. Place in the slow cooker (if you have used a separate pan).

Stir in the chickpeas, tomatoes, stock and coconut cream, then season with salt and pepper. Cover and cook on low for 4 hours, until the aubergine is meltingly tender but still holding its shape.

Ladle into bowls and garnish with the coriander. Serve with poppadums, mango chutney and tzatziki, if liked.

15 MINS + SOAKING OVERNIGHT

 7¼ HRS

 FREEZER FRIENDLY

225g (8oz) dried haricot beans

1 large onion, chopped

2 large carrots, sliced

2 celery sticks, chopped

2 ripe tomatoes, cut into wedges

6 garlic cloves, peeled

100g (4oz) smoked bacon lardons

1.2 litres (2 pints) chicken stock
(from a cube is fine)

4 confit duck legs (see the intro)

100g (4oz) piece of saucisson or any
dry-cured Continental sausage, cut
into bite-sized chunks

1 bouquet garni (bay leaf, thyme,
rosemary, sage)

75g (3oz) fresh ciabatta
breadcrumbs

2 tbsp chopped fresh flat-leaf
parsley

sea salt and freshly ground black
pepper

TO GARNISH

fresh thyme leaves

Neven's Slow Cooker Cassoulet
Serves 4-6

This is much less complicated than the traditional French version but still has that great depth of flavour. The Dunnes Stores Simply Better range includes incredible cooked duck confits, as does Silver Hill, making this easy enough to cook for a busy weeknight.

Soak the beans in plenty of cold water overnight, then drain.

Put the beans, onion, carrots, celery, tomatoes, garlic and bacon in a slow cooker and stir to combine. Season with salt and pepper and pour in the stock. Tuck in the duck confit legs, saucisson and the bouquet garni. Cover and cook on a low heat for 7 hours, until the duck confit are meltingly tender and the beans are soft and creamy.

Switch off the slow cooker and carefully lift out the inner bowl. Mix the breadcrumbs with the parsley and season with salt and pepper. Scatter over the cassoulet and flash under the grill until bubbling and golden brown. Garnish with fresh thyme leaves and serve straight to the table to allow everyone to help themselves.

25 MINS

 4½ HRS

 LOADS OF VEG

 FREEZER FRIENDLY

4 tbsp rapeseed oil

2 large onions, roughly chopped

4 garlic cloves, finely chopped

1 × 2.5cm (1in) piece of fresh root
ginger, peeled and finely chopped

2 tbsp mild curry powder or paste
(I love the Dunnes Stores Simply
Better Mild Curry Seasoning)

2 tsp ground turmeric

2 tsp ground cinnamon

2 × 400g (14oz) tins of Italian
chopped tomatoes

500g (1lb 2oz) boneless, skinless
chicken cubes (thigh or breast)

1 butternut squash, peeled,
deseeded and cut into cubes

2 tbsp clear honey

about 450ml (¾ pint) chicken stock
(from a cube is fine)

sea salt and freshly ground black
pepper

TO GARNISH

chopped fresh mint and/or coriander

roughly chopped toasted pistachio
nuts

TO SERVE

couscous

natural yoghurt

Moroccan Chicken Tagine with Butternut Squash Serves 4–6

I like to make this with chicken thighs, but I'd always get my butcher to prep them for me by removing the skin, trimming them and removing the bones. Otherwise breasts also work well, and because the heat of the slow cooker is so gentle, they stay nice and moist. Use pumpkin instead of the butternut squash if it's in season.

Preheat your slow cooker according to the manufacturer's instructions. If your slow cooker has a sauté option, you can use this; if not, use a large sauté pan on the hob over a medium heat. Heat the oil, then add the onions and sauté for 8–10 minutes, stirring occasionally, until they are softened and have taken on a little colour.

Add the garlic and ginger and sauté for another 3–4 minutes. Stir in the curry powder or paste, turmeric and cinnamon and cook for 1 minute. Pour in the tomatoes and carefully blend to a thick purée with a hand-held blender. Using a spatula, transfer to the slow cooker (if you have used a separate pan).

Stir the chicken into the tomato base along with the butternut squash and honey, adding enough stock to make a thick-ish sauce that barely covers all the ingredients. Season with salt and pepper. Cover and cook on low for 4 hours, until the chicken and butternut squash are completely tender.

When ready to serve, make the couscous according to the packet instructions and spoon into wide-rimmed bowls. Ladle over the tagine and add a dollop of yoghurt to each one, then scatter the herbs and pistachio nuts on top to garnish.

30 MINS

 9½ HRS

❄ FREEZER FRIENDLY (PORK)

2.5kg (5½lb) pork shoulder on the bone (you can ask your butcher to saw the leg bone to make it fit into the slow cooker)

200ml (7fl oz) apple cider vinegar

75g (3oz) dark muscovado sugar

2 cinnamon sticks

2 star anise

2 tbsp Highbank Organic Orchard Syrup (or use any organic apple syrup)

1 tbsp black or Szechuan peppercorns

1 tbsp tomato purée

2 tsp dried chilli flakes

2 tsp dark soy sauce

1 heaped tsp sea salt flakes

TO SERVE

demi-baguettes, split in half lengthways

pomegranate and herb salad

garlic mayonnaise

Pulled Pork Sandwich
Serves 8-10

This is one of those mega meals that's perfect if you're looking for an easy entertaining option. It can be made up to three days in advance, so all you need to do is reheat it gently on the day. Please don't be put off by the length of time it takes to cook – the nine-hour wait is all hands-off cooking time and is possibly the most worthwhile nine hours you'll ever spend!

Put a large ridged griddle pan on a high heat. When it's smoking hot, lay the pork on top and cook for about 8 minutes, turning as you go. For the last 2 minutes of the cooking time, cover with a large sheet of foil so that the resulting smoke infuses the meat.

Preheat your slow cooker according to the manufacturer's instructions. Add the vinegar, sugar, cinnamon, star anise, apple syrup, peppercorns, tomato purée, chilli flakes, soy sauce and salt and heat on high, stirring until the sugar has dissolved. Reduce the heat to low, then remove 4 tablespoons of the sauce and set it aside in a ramekin.

Add the pork to the slow cooker. Cover and cook on low for 9 hours, until the meat can easily be pulled off the bone. Transfer the pork to a large platter to cool a little.

When cool enough to handle, pull off and discard the bones and fatty skin, then shred the meat into bite-sized pieces and stir in the reserved sauce. This will now sit happily in the fridge for up to three days and can be reheated in the oven at 220°C (425°F/gas mark 7) for 35–45 minutes, until piping hot.

Split the baguettes and add some of the pomegranate and herb salad with a smear of garlic mayonnaise. Top with the pulled pork and arrange on plates to serve.

20 MINS

 3½ HRS

 FREEZER FRIENDLY

Ratatouille and Aubergine Lasagne with Buffalo Mozzarella Serves 4–6

2 tbsp rapeseed oil

2 onions, sliced

4 garlic cloves, finely chopped

2 large courgettes, diced (about 400g (14oz))

1 red pepper, thinly sliced

1 yellow pepper, thinly sliced

1 × 400g (14oz) tin of Italian chopped tomatoes

2 tbsp sun-dried tomato purée

½ vegetable stock cube, crumbled

15g (½oz) fresh basil

1 large aubergine, thinly sliced lengthways

6 lasagne sheets

500g (1lb 2oz) buffalo mozzarella, cut into cubes

This a great vegetarian dish that cooks beautifully in the slow cooker. It uses a simple ratatouille, which gets layered up with slices of aubergine and lasagne sheets. Buy the best buffalo mozzarella you can find – Toonsbridge is a particular favourite of mine.

Preheat your slow cooker according to the manufacturer's instructions.

Heat the oil in a large frying pan over a medium heat. Add the onions and garlic and sauté for 5 minutes, until softened. Add the courgettes, peppers, tomatoes, sun-dried tomato purée and stock cube. Season with salt and pepper, then cover and simmer for 5 minutes. Don't be tempted to add any more liquid, as plenty of moisture will come from the vegetables once they start cooking. Strip the leaves from the basil sprigs and tear most of them in, reserving some to garnish.

Arrange half of the aubergine slices in the bottom of the slow cooker and cover with half of the lasagne sheets, breaking them up to fit as necessary. Add one-third of the ratatouille, then cover with the rest of the aubergine slices. Add the remaining lasagne sheets and finish with the rest of the ratatouille. Cover and cook on high for 3 hours, until the vegetables and pasta are tender. Turn off the slow cooker.

Preheat the grill to high. Scatter over the mozzarella, then flash under the hot grill for 5 minutes, until the mozzarella has melted into the ratatouille. Scatter over the rest of the basil and arrange on plates to serve.

15 MINS

 7½ HRS

 FREEZER FIRENDLY (LAMB)

Fragrant Pulled Lamb with Carrot and Tomato Salad
Serves 4-6

2 tbsp rapeseed oil

1 large onion, thinly sliced

1 garlic bulb, cloves peeled

1 × 2.5cm (1in) piece of fresh root ginger, peeled and shredded into matchsticks

2 tbsp paprika

2 tbsp ground cumin

1 tbsp ground coriander

2 tsp garam masala

1 tsp cayenne pepper

225ml (8fl oz) apple cider vinegar

1 boned and rolled lamb shoulder

sea salt and freshly ground black pepper

FOR THE SALAD

3 carrots, cut into julienne

2 ripe tomatoes, finely chopped

1 red onion, finely chopped

good handful of fresh coriander leaves

juice of 1 lime, plus extra wedges to serve

1 tbsp rapeseed oil

TO SERVE

white flatbreads

shop-bought tzatziki

mango chutney

A boned and rolled lamb shoulder is great value for money, and cooked slowly in a rich, spicy gravy makes it so delicious that you'll be dreaming about it. I love the small flatbreads that puff up as you reheat them – I normally do mine directly on the gas hob, but you can also do them in the oven or under the grill.

Preheat your slow cooker according to the manufacturer's instructions. If your slow cooker has a sauté option, you can use this; if not, use a sauté pan on the hob over a medium heat. Heat the 2 tablespoons of rapeseed oil, then add the onion, garlic and ginger and fry for about 10 minutes. Stir in the spices and pour in the vinegar, stirring to combine.

Place in the slow cooker (if you have used a separate pan). Season with salt and pepper. Add the lamb shoulder, skin side down. Cover and cook on low for 7 hours, until the lamb is meltingly tender.

Remove the lamb shoulder from the slow cooker and cut off the string. Take off the skin and any sinew, then shred the meat with two forks. Skim off all the fat from the juices, then stir them back into the shredded meat.

When ready to serve, mix together the carrots, tomatoes, red onion and coriander. Dress with the lime juice and rapeseed oil.

Arrange some of the meat mixture and salad on one side of each flatbread, then top with the tzatziki and mango chutney. Serve with lime wedges for squeezing over, then fold over and eat with your hands.

30 MINS

 8½ HRS

 FREEZER FRIENDLY (RIBS)

2 garlic cloves, crushed

4 tbsp clear honey

3 tbsp light muscovado sugar

3 tbsp soy sauce

3 tbsp hoisin sauce

3 tbsp rice wine vinegar

2 tbsp freshly grated root ginger

1.5–2kg (3lb 5oz–4½lb) meaty pork ribs

1 litre (1¾ pints) water

20g (¾oz) fresh coriander

FOR THE SLAW

100g (4oz) red cabbage, cored and finely shredded

100g (4oz) white cabbage, cored and finely shredded

1 large carrot, grated

2 tbsp rapeseed oil

1 tbsp sesame oil

1 tbsp rice wine vinegar

1 tsp caster sugar

1 tsp salt

TO GARNISH

spring onion curls (optional)

Char Sui Pork Ribs with Slaw
Serves 4–6

These ribs are so tender that the meat literally falls off the bone. I like to finish them off in the oven or barbecue for that really sticky glaze. The easiest way to make the slaw is with a fine grater attachment on a food processor, which can be done in advance and kept in the fridge for three days – just add the coriander at the last minute.

Mix the garlic in a bowl with the honey, muscovado sugar, soy sauce, hoisin, rice wine vinegar and ginger. Spoon 4 tablespoons of the marinade into the slow cooker (reserving the remainder) and add the ribs. Top up with the water, mixing to combine. Strip the leaves off the coriander and set them aside for the slaw, then put the stalks into the slow cooker. Cover and cook on low for 8 hours, until the ribs are tender but not falling off the bone.

Preheat the oven to 220°C (425°F/gas mark 7). Line a large baking tray with foil.

Remove the ribs from the slow cooker using a slotted spoon or tongs. Handle them carefully, as the meat will be very tender and may start to fall off the bone. Baste with the reserved marinade and lay on the foil-lined tray. Cook in the preheated oven for 25–30 minutes, until starting to crisp on the outside.

Meanwhile, to make the slaw, mix the red and white cabbage with the carrot and reserved coriander leaves. Put the rapeseed oil, sesame oil, rice wine vinegar, caster sugar and salt in a screw-topped jar and shake until evenly combined, then use to dress the slaw.

If making the spring onion curls, cut the spring onions into very thin slices, then put in a bowl of ice-cold water to curl. Drain well and lightly pat dry on kitchen paper before using.

Arrange the slaw on plates with the char sui pork ribs and garnish with the spring onion curls (if using).

15 MINS

 6 HRS + 50 MINS RESTING

 FREEZER FRIENDLY

1.5–1.8kg (3¼–4lb) unsmoked boneless gammon joint, soaked (see the intro)

1 litre (1¾ pints) dry cider

1 onion, sliced

1 celery stick, roughly chopped

1 carrot, roughly chopped

1 bouquet garni (bay leaf, thyme, rosemary, sage)

2 star anise

1 cinnamon stick

2 tsp black peppercorns

FOR THE GLAZE

175g (6oz) blackcurrant preserves

100g (4oz) light muscovado sugar

juice of 2 clementines

4 star anise

TO SERVE

Asian-style stir-fried greens (optional)

Gammon with Blackcurrant and Star Anise Glaze Serves 10-12

Ask your butcher if they think the gammon needs to be soaked. Normally at least 6 hours in cold water or overnight is best to remove any excess salt from the curing process. If you buy it in the supermarket, I would always soak it – better to be safe than sorry!

Preheat your slow cooker according to the manufacturer's instructions. Add the gammon joint and pour over the cider. Add the onion, celery, carrot, bouquet garni, star anise, cinnamon and peppercorns. Cover and cook on low for 5 hours, until the gammon is tender but still holding its shape. Lift out the joint and leave to rest for 30 minutes or you can now leave it for one to two days before finishing the recipe.

Preheat the oven to 190°C (375°F/gas mark 5). Line a roasting tin with foil.

To make the glaze, put the blackcurrant preserves in a small pan with the sugar, clementine juice and star anise. Heat gently until the sugar has dissolved, then simmer for 3–4 minutes, until reduced to a thick glaze, stirring to ensure it doesn't catch at the bottom.

Carefully peel away the skin from the gammon joint, leaving the layer of white fat intact. Using a sharp knife, score the fat diagonally into a diamond pattern, being careful not to cut into the meat. Put into the foil-lined roasting tin, then brush over half of the glaze. Roast in the preheated oven for 15 minutes, then pour over the rest of the glaze, including the star anise, and roast for another 30 minutes, until golden and sticky.

Transfer the gammon to a platter and leave to rest for 15–20 minutes, spooning over the sticky glaze every few minutes until it has all stuck to the joint. Carve into slices and arrange on plates with some Asian-style stir-fried greens, if liked.

30 MINS

 8½ HRS

 FREEZER FRIENDLY

1 tbsp rapeseed oil

450g (1lb) stewing lamb pieces, well trimmed (if it has bones in it, add another 225g (8oz) to the weight)

100g (4oz) smoked streaky bacon lardons

1 large onion, sliced

4 carrots, cut into big chunks

1 small turnip, cut into chunks

6 potatoes, cut into chunks

2 bay leaves

2 tsp fresh thyme leaves

1.2 litres (2 pints) chicken stock (from a cube is fine) or water

50g (2oz) pearl barley

1 large leek, trimmed and sliced

knob of butter

sea salt and freshly ground black pepper

Irish Lamb Hotpot
Serves 4-6

Ask at the butcher counter for stewing lamb – I like middle neck or scrag, but gigot chops are also delicious. They're cooked on the bone, so the flavour is intense. However, if you don't fancy the bones, ready-prepared stewing lamb pieces are an excellent option.

Preheat your slow cooker according to the manufacturer's instructions. If your slow cooker has a sauté option, you can use this; if not, use a sauté pan on the hob. Heat the oil over a medium heat, then add the lamb and brown all over, turning regularly. Add the bacon and sauté for a few minutes, until sizzling. Place in a slow cooker (if you have used a separate pan).

Add the onion, carrots, turnip, potatoes, bay leaves, thyme and enough of the stock or water to just cover. Season with salt and pepper. Cover and cook on low for 6 hours.

Stir in the pearl barley and leek, then raise the temperature to high and cook for 2 hours more, until the pearl barley is tender.

Stir in the butter just before serving, then ladle into warmed bowls and add a good grinding of black pepper to serve.

30 MINS

 5¼ HRS

 LOADS OF VEG

 FREEZER FRIENDLY

2 tbsp rapeseed oil

2 onions, finely chopped

2 garlic cloves, finely chopped

1 fresh green chilli, deseeded and finely chopped

1 tbsp finely grated root ginger

2 tsp garam masala

2 tsp ground turmeric

½–1 tsp cayenne pepper (to taste)

1 small Crown Prince pumpkin, peeled, deseeded and cut into cubes (about 500g (1lb 2oz))

550g (1¼lb) boneless, skinless chicken fillets, cut into 2.5cm (1in) cubes

1 × 400g (14oz) tin of Italian chopped tomatoes

225g (8oz) green lentils, well rinsed

600ml (1 pint) water

1 × 400ml (14fl oz) tin of coconut milk

2 tbsp mango chutney, plus extra to serve

1 tbsp tomato purée

sea salt and freshly ground black pepper

TO GARNISH

handful of fresh coriander leaves

handful of fresh mint leaves

TO SERVE

wraps or warmed naan bread

Chicken and Pumpkin Dhansak
Serves 4-6

This traditional Indian curry has its origins in Persian and Gujarati cuisine. If pumpkins aren't available, substitute with butternut squash or sweet potatoes. This is quite filling so it needs very little to serve alongside it, although I do like some coconut naan or even just a couple of warmed puffed-up wraps to help scoop it up.

Preheat your slow cooker according to the manufacturer's instructions. If your slow cooker has a sauté option, you can use this; if not, use a large sauté pan on the hob over a medium heat. Heat the oil, then add the onions and garlic and sauté for about 10 minutes, until lightly golden. Place in the slow cooker (if you have used a separate pan).

Stir in the green chilli, ginger and spices, then add the rest of the ingredients. Stir well to combine, then cover and cook on low for 5 hours, until the chicken and lentils are completely tender.

Spoon the chicken and pumpkin dhansak onto warmed plates and scatter over the coriander and mint leaves to garnish. Place the wraps or naan breads in a separate dish to pass around at the table along with the mango chutney.

45 MINS + MARINATING OVERNIGHT

 7½ HRS + 20 MINS RESTING

 FREEZER FRIENDLY (PORK)

1 × 1.8kg (4lb) pork butt roast (ask your butcher for the upper part of the shoulder from the front leg)

1 × 200g (7oz) tin of crushed pineapple in natural juice, drained

1 small onion, chopped

15g (½oz) fresh coriander

juice of 1 small orange

2 tbsp granulated garlic

2 tbsp chipotle paste (or use 1 tbsp smoked paprika and 1 tbsp Tabasco instead)

1 tbsp white wine vinegar

1 tsp dried oregano

1 tsp ground cumin

1 tbsp rapeseed oil

4 tbsp water

sea salt and freshly ground black pepper

TO SERVE

small warm soft corn tortillas

thinly sliced radishes

fresh coriander leaves

salsa verde (shop-bought)

lime wedges

Pork Tacos al Pastor
Serves 6-8

Besides adding some sweetness and acidity, the pineapple also has an enzyme called bromelain that breaks down proteins, which makes the meat very tender.

Place the pork in the freezer for about 30 minutes, until it's firm enough to cut.

Meanwhile, to make the marinade, place the rest of the ingredients except the oil and water in a food processor, season generously with salt and pepper and blitz to a purée.

Take the pork out of the freezer and place on a chopping board, fat side up. Cut into slices 1cm (½in) thick, almost but not quite all the way through. Slather the marinade between each layer, then tie the roast back together with butcher's string. Place in a shallow non-metallic container and cover loosely with cling film. Place in the fridge overnight to marinate.

The next day, bring the pork back to room temperature, then preheat your slow cooker according to the manufacturer's instructions. If your slow cooker has a sauté option, you can use this; if not, use a large sauté pan on the hob over a medium heat. Heat the oil, then add the pork and cook until lightly browned and sizzling. Place in the slow cooker, fat side up (if you have used a separate pan), along with the juices and the water. Cover and cook on low for 7 hours, until the pork is tender.

Remove the pork from the slow cooker and cover with tin foil, then leave to rest for 20 minutes.

When ready to serve, cut the meat up into small pieces and place in a bowl, moistening with some of the juices. Fill the tortillas with the pork, then top with the radishes, coriander and salsa verde. Arrange on plates and serve with the lime wedges.

30 MINS + SOAKING OVERNIGHT

 8½ HRS

 LOADS OF VEG

 FREEZER FRIENDLY

225g (8oz) dried butter beans

2 tbsp rapeseed oil

2 onions, finely chopped

2 carrots, finely diced

2 celery sticks, finely diced

200g (7oz) mushrooms, finely diced

350g (12oz) lean minced beef

350g (12oz) lean minced pork

300ml (½ pint) red wine

2 × 400g (14oz) tins of Italian whole plum tomatoes

1 bouquet garni (bay leaf, thyme, rosemary, sage)

about 600ml (1 pint) chicken stock (from a cube is fine)

675–900g (1½–2lb) spaghetti

sea salt and freshly ground black pepper

TO SERVE

freshly shaved Parmesan cheese

Ragù alla Bolognese with Butter Beans Serves 8–12

There's no doubt that making an authentic Bolognese can take a bit of time, which is why I'll always make a large quantity so that I can freeze it in smaller batches. It's perfect for making in a slow cooker, as it really draws off the flavour and makes the meat incredibly tender.

Soak the beans in plenty of cold water overnight, then drain.

Preheat your slow cooker according to the manufacturer's instructions. If your slow cooker has a sauté option, you can use this; if not, use a large sauté pan on the hob over a medium heat. Heat the oil, then add the onions, carrots, celery and mushrooms. Cook for 8–10 minutes, stirring occasionally, until the vegetables have softened and taken on a little colour.

Add the minced beef and pork and mix until well combined, then sauté until well browned, breaking up any lumps with a wooden spoon. Deglaze the pan with a little of the red wine, scraping the bottom of the pan to remove any browned bits. Pour in the remaining wine along with the plum tomatoes and break them up using a wooden spoon. Place in the slow cooker (if you have used a separate pan), including the juices.

Add the butter beans and bouquet garni and season with salt and pepper. Pour in the stock, stirring to combine. Cover and cook on low for 8 hours, until the meat and beans are meltingly tender.

When ready to serve, cook the spaghetti in a pan of boiling salted water for 10–12 minutes, until al dente (tender but still with a little bite). Add to the ragù, tossing until well combined, then divide between warmed bowls. Scatter over the Parmesan shavings and add a good grinding of black pepper to serve.

30 MINS

 3½ HRS

 LOADS OF VEG

Vietnamese Meatball and Sweet Potato Bowl Serves 4–6

250g (9oz) minced lamb

225g (8oz) lean minced pork

50g (2oz) fresh white breadcrumbs

1 onion, very finely chopped

1 egg, lightly beaten

1 fresh red chilli, deseeded and finely chopped

4 tbsp chopped fresh coriander

1 tbsp dark soy sauce

1 tbsp Thai fish sauce (nam pla)

1 × 5cm (2in) piece of fresh root ginger, peeled and finely chopped

1 tbsp rapeseed oil

300ml (½ pint) chicken stock (from a cube is fine)

1 × 400g (14oz) tin of Italian chopped tomatoes

250ml (9fl oz) coconut cream

2 tbsp mild curry powder or paste (I love the Dunnes Stores Simply Better Mild Curry Seasoning)

1 large sweet potato, peeled and cut into batons

TO GARNISH

black and white sesame seeds

lime wedges

TO SERVE

small cucumber ribbons

curled carrot ribbons

fresh mint or coriander leaves

Once you've added the embellishments, this bowl transports you straight to South-East Asia, where they put a huge amount of effort into the visual impact of a Buddha-inspired bowl. The balance of flavours and textures will have you returning to this recipe time and time again.

Preheat your slow cooker according to the manufacturer's instructions.

Place the minced lamb and pork in a bowl with the breadcrumbs, onion, egg, chilli, coriander, soy, fish sauce and half of the ginger. Mix to combine and shape into 12 even-sized balls.

If your slow cooker has a sauté option, you can use this; if not, use a large sauté pan on the hob over a medium heat. Heat the oil, then add the meatballs and cook for about 10 minutes, until lightly golden. Place in the slow cooker (if you have used a separate pan). Pour in the stock, scraping the bottom of the pan to remove any browned bits, then stir in the tomatoes, coconut cream, curry powder or paste and the rest of the ginger. Add the sweet potato batons and cover, then cook on low for 3 hours, until the meatballs and sweet potato batons are tender but still holding their shape.

Using a tongs, arrange the meatballs in bowls and sprinkle with the sesame seeds, then add the sweet potato batons alongside. Add some cucumber and carrot ribbons and mint or coriander. Garnish with the lime wedges to serve.

20 MINS

 5½ HRS + 20 MINS RESTING

 LOADS OF VEG

Pot Roasted Chicken with Green Butter and Root Vegetables Serves 4–6

1 large chicken (preferably free-range or organic)

2 small leeks, sliced

2 carrots, sliced

2 parsnips, cut into batons

1 small turnip, cut into batons

4 tbsp dry white wine

2 tbsp chicken stock (from a cube is fine)

sea salt and freshly ground black pepper

FOR THE GREEN BUTTER

50g (2oz) butter, at room temperature

2 garlic cloves, crushed

2 tbsp chopped fresh mixed herbs (flat-leaf parsley, tarragon and basil)

TO GARNISH

chopped fresh flat-leaf parsley

TO SERVE

French baguette

Pot roasting is a great way to keep chicken succulent and the bed of vegetables imparts loads of flavour. If you want the skin to be browned, simply grill it for a couple of minutes at the end.

Preheat your slow cooker according to the manufacturer's instructions.

To make the green butter, mix the butter in a small bowl with the garlic and herbs and season with salt and pepper. Gently ease the skin away from the chicken breast and push the green butter underneath.

Place the leeks, carrots, parsnips and turnip in the base of the slow cooker, pour over the wine and stock and season with salt and pepper. Sit the chicken on top and cover with the lid. Cook on low for 5 hours, then check that the chicken is cooked by wiggling the wing – it should feel very loose. If you would like more colour on the chicken skin, simply flash it under a hot grill for 3–4 minutes, until lightly browned.

Tip the chicken up so that any liquid flows out, then transfer to a carving board and cover with foil. Leave to rest for 20 minutes, then carve into slices.

Increase the heat on the slow cooker to high and cook the vegetables with the juices for another 30 minutes, until slightly reduced and glazed.

Garnish with the parsley, then serve straight to the table with some French baguette.

20 MINS + SOAKING OVERNIGHT

 10½ HRS

 LOADS OF VEG

 FREEZER FRIENDLY

225g (8oz) dried black turtle beans

2 tbsp rapeseed oil

2 onions, finely chopped

2 celery sticks, finely chopped

1 large green pepper, finely diced

1 tbsp dark brown sugar

500g (1lb 2oz) rump steak, trimmed and diced into 1cm (½in) cubes

3 garlic cloves, crushed

2 tbsp Cajun seasoning (I like the Dunnes Stores Simply Better Organic Cajun Spice Seasoning)

600ml (1 pint) beef or chicken stock (from a cube is fine)

2 × 400g (14oz) tins of Italian chopped tomatoes

2 tbsp tomato purée

sea salt and freshly ground black pepper

TO SERVE

tortilla chips

lime wedges

fresh coriander leaves

soured cream

guacamole

Sriracha hot chilli sauce

Family-Style Beef Chilli
Serves 4–6

Ask your butcher to prepare the rump steak for you or ask them what other cuts they have that might be suitable, as any braising meat is perfect for this type of cooking. Serve with tortilla chips, soured cream, guacamole and hot chilli sauce, depending on what you fancy.

Soak the beans in plenty of cold water overnight, then drain.

Preheat your slow cooker according to the manufacturer's instructions. If your slow cooker has a sauté option, you can use this; if not, use a large sauté pan on the hob over a medium heat. Heat the oil, then add the onions, celery, green pepper and sugar. Cook for 15–20 minutes, stirring from time to time, until golden and well caramelised. Don't be tempted to decrease the amount of time this takes, as this is very important for the flavour.

Add the beef and mix until well combined, then sauté for another few minutes, until well browned. Stir in the garlic and Cajun seasoning. Deglaze the pan with a little of the stock, scraping the bottom of the pan to remove any browned bits. Pour in the remaining stock along with the tomatoes and tomato purée and break up using a wooden spoon. Place in the slow cooker (if you have used a separate pan), including the juices.

Season well with salt and pepper and stir in the black beans. Cover and cook on low for 10 hours, until the meat and beans are meltingly tender.

Serve bowls of the beef chilli with tortilla chips, lime wedges and fresh coriander leaves. Pass around the soured cream, guacamole and chilli sauce separately so that everyone can help themselves.

15 MINS

 7¾ HRS

❄ FREEZER FRIENDLY

1 tbsp rapeseed oil

4–6 lamb shanks

large knob of butter

2 onions, sliced

4 garlic cloves, crushed

pared rind and juice of 1 small lemon

1 tbsp ground cumin

2 tsp ground coriander

2 tsp ground cinnamon

1 tsp ground ginger

good pinch of saffron strands or ground turmeric (optional)

3 star anise

2 tbsp tomato purée

1 tbsp clear honey

600ml (1 pint) lamb or chicken stock (from a cube is fine)

3 firm Conference pears, peeled, halved and cored

sea salt and freshly ground black pepper

TO GARNISH

pomegranate seeds

fresh mint leaves

TO SERVE

couscous

Sweet Spiced Lamb Shanks with Pears Serves 4–6

Once the lamb shanks are cooked the sauce will be fairly thin, so if you prefer a thicker stew, remove the lamb and pears, then blend the sauce with a hand-held blender – the onions will thicken the sauce beautifully.

Preheat your slow cooker according to the manufacturer's instructions. If your slow cooker has a sauté option, you can use this; if not, use a sauté pan on the hob and heat the oil over a medium heat. Season the lamb shanks, then brown in the hot oil for about 10 minutes, turning regularly, until nicely browned all over. Set aside on a plate.

Add the butter to the pan, then add the onions and sauté for 10–15 minutes, until golden. Stir in the garlic, lemon rind and spices and cook for 1 minute. Place in a slow cooker (if you have used a separate pan). Stir in the star anise, tomato purée and honey, then add the stock and half of the lemon juice.

Nestle the shanks into the slow cooker, then add the pear quarters in and around the meat and season with salt and pepper. Cover and cook on low for 7 hours, until the lamb shanks are meltingly tender. Season to taste with the rest of the lemon juice.

When ready to serve, make the couscous according to the packet instructions. Spoon into wide-rimmed bowls and place a lamb shank and pieces of pear in each one, then ladle over the sauce. Garnish with the pomegranate seeds and mint leaves to serve.

30 MINS

 5½ HRS

 LOADS OF VEG

 FREEZER FRIENDLY

1 tbsp rapeseed oil

450g (1lb) minced lamb

2 rindless smoked streaky bacon rashers, finely chopped

4 carrots, diced

2 leeks, finely chopped

2 celery sticks, finely chopped

225g (8oz) green lentils, well rinsed

1 tbsp tomato purée

1 tsp chopped fresh thyme, plus extra to garnish

1 heaped tbsp plain flour

900ml (1½ pints) chicken stock (from a cube is fine)

2 tbsp Worcestershire sauce

1kg (2¼lb) potatoes, cut into cubes

100ml (3½fl oz) milk

25g (1oz) butter

sea salt and freshly ground black pepper

Shepherd's Pie with Green Lentils Serves 4-6

These days I'm trying to pack as much vegetables into our family dinners as possible. We still eat meat, but now I prefer to bulk it out with loads of vegetables and pulses, such as the green lentils I'm using in this dish. It immediately becomes much more nutritionally balanced with no extra effort.

Preheat your slow cooker according to the manufacturer's instructions. If your slow cooker has a sauté option, you can use this; if not, use a non-stick large sauté pan on the hob over a medium heat. Heat the oil, then tip in the lamb and bacon and sauté for about 5 minutes to brown, breaking up any lumps with a wooden spoon.

Add the carrots, leeks and celery and cook for 4–5 minutes, until softened. Stir in the lentils, tomato purée and thyme, then sprinkle over the flour and cook for 1 minute, stirring. Pour in the stock and Worcestershire sauce and season with salt and pepper. Place in the slow cooker (if you have used a separate pan).

Meanwhile, steam the potatoes for 12–14 minutes, until tender. Mash well, then beat in the milk and butter. Season to taste. Gently spoon the potatoes on top of the mince and lentil mixture.

Cover and cook on low for 5 hours, until the lentils are completely tender and the lamb mixture is bubbling up the sides. Crisp up the potato topping under the grill if you like. Garnish with fresh thyme leaves to serve.

25 MINS

 8½ HRS

 LOADS OF VEG

 FREEZER FRIENDLY

2 onions, cut into wedges

50g (2oz) fresh root ginger, peeled and thickly sliced

4 whole cloves

3 star anise

2 tbsp coriander seeds

1 turkey carcass (or 2–3 chicken carcasses, depending on their size), all meat removed

3 tbsp Thai fish sauce (nam pla)

2 tbsp muscovado sugar (light or dark is fine)

250g (9oz) flat rice noodles

400g (14oz) cooked turkey or chicken, sliced or shredded

100g (4oz) fresh bean sprouts

2 large carrots, cut into julienne

1 courgette, cut into julienne

TO GARNISH

fresh Thai basil, mint and coriander leaves

thinly sliced fresh red chillies

TO SERVE

lime wedges

chilli oil (optional)

Slow Cooker Turkey Pho
Serves 4–6

This is a great way to use up leftover turkey at Christmas, but you can also use a couple of chicken carcasses. We always buy a good-quality organic or free-range chicken for a Sunday roast, then just pop the carcass into a bag and freeze until we want to use it. It's a brilliant recipe if you haven't got time to make stock but feel guilty throwing out the carcass.

Preheat your slow cooker according to the manufacturer's instructions. If your slow cooker has a sauté option, you can use this; if not, use a large non-stick sauté pan on the hob over a high heat. Dry fry the onions and ginger for 6–8 minutes, until the onions are soft and lightly caramelised. Add the spices and cook for a few minutes, until fragrant. Place in the slow cooker (if you have used a separate pan).

Break up the turkey or chicken carcasses, then pour in enough boiling water to ensure the bones are completely covered, being careful not to overfill it. Cover with a lid and cook on low for 8 hours, until you have a fragrant stock.

Strain the stock, discarding the bones and spices. Season with the fish sauce and sugar, stirring to combine, and taste to make sure you're happy with the balance of flavours. To freeze for later, leave to cool completely and freeze in an airtight container for up to three months. Alternatively, pour the stock back into the slow cooker and keep warm.

Prepare the noodles by placing them in a large heatproof bowl and pouring over enough just-boiled water to cover, then leave to soak for 4 minutes, until softened, or according to the packet instructions. Drain and rinse under cold running water.

Divide the noodles between bowls and scatter over the cooked turkey or chicken and bean sprouts along with the carrot and courgette. Ladle over the flavoured stock and finish with the herbs and chillies. Serve with lime wedges and chilli oil (if using).

20 MINS + SOAKING OVERNIGHT

 9¼ HRS

 LOADS OF VEG

 FREEZER FRIENDLY

225g (8oz) dried cannellini beans

25g (1oz) plain flour

500g (1lb 2oz) stewing beef pieces

2 tbsp rapeseed oil

1 large onion, chopped

4 large carrots, halved and cut into thick batons

2 celery sticks, cut into thick batons

1 × 400g (14oz) tin of Italian chopped tomatoes

1 litre (1¾ pints) chicken stock (from a cube is fine)

2 tbsp tomato purée

1 tbsp Worcestershire sauce

1 tsp za'atar seasoning (or similar – see the intro)

sea salt and freshly ground black pepper

TO SERVE

roughly chopped fresh flat-leaf parsley

chunks of sourdough baguette

Braised Beef with Carrots and Cannellini Beans Serves 4-6

Za'atar is a fragrant Middle Eastern seasoning mix that instantly adds a wonderful savoury spice to any dish. If you want to make your own, just mix equal quantities of ground cumin, sesame seeds, dried oregano and sumac (wine-coloured dried berries that add a lemon-lime tartness with an exotic twist).

Soak the beans in plenty of cold water overnight, then drain.

Preheat your slow cooker according to the manufacturer's instructions. Season the flour and put in a large ziplock bag. Add the stewing beef pieces and shake to coat, then remove, dusting off any excess flour.

If your slow cooker has a sauté option, you can use this; if not, use a sauté pan on the hob over a medium heat. Heat the rapeseed oil, then add the beef and cook until browned, turning regularly. Place in the slow cooker (if you have used a separate pan), including any juices.

Add the remaining ingredients to the slow cooker and season with salt and pepper. Set to low, cover and cook for 9 hours, until the beef and cannellini beans are meltingly tender. Scatter over the parsley and serve with chunks of sourdough baguette.

15 MINS + SOAKING OVERNIGHT

 9¼ HRS

 FREEZER FRIENDLY

225g (8oz) dried butter beans

2 tbsp rapeseed oil

1.2kg (2½lb) shoulder of lamb, well trimmed and cut into 4cm (1½in) pieces

2 onions, thinly sliced

6 garlic cloves, peeled and halved

2 tsp chopped fresh sage

1 tsp chopped fresh thyme

1 tsp dried chilli flakes

2 × 400g (14oz) tins of whole Italian plum tomatoes

1 tbsp red wine vinegar

1 tsp caster sugar

1 litre (1¾ pints) chicken stock (from a cube is fine)

100g (4oz) feta cheese

sea salt and freshly ground black pepper

TO GARNISH

roughly chopped fresh flat-leaf parsley

Greek Lamb with Butter Beans and Tomatoes Serves 4-6

Preparing lamb shoulder into cubes requires a bit of work and the supermarkets tend to only sell them boned and rolled, so it's worth making a trip to your local butcher for this. Ring ahead and they'll have it waiting for you. This cut shouldn't cost you much more than a tenner.

Soak the beans in plenty of cold water overnight, then drain.

Preheat your slow cooker according to the manufacturer's instructions. If your slow cooker has a sauté option, you can use this; if not, use a large sauté pan on the hob over a medium-high heat. Heat the oil, then add the lamb pieces and sauté for 3–4 minutes, until just sealed. Toss in the onions and garlic and continue to cook for another few minutes, until everything is beginning to catch a bit of colour. Place in the slow cooker (if you have used a separate pan).

Add the herbs and chilli flakes to the lamb mixture. Break up the tomatoes with your hands, then stir them in along with the butter beans, vinegar and sugar. Pour in the stock and season with salt and pepper, stirring well to combine. Cover and cook on low for 9 hours, until the lamb is meltingly tender and the butter beans are soft.

Ladle the stew into shallow bowls and crumble over the feta cheese. Garnish with parsley to serve.

15 MINS

 5½ HRS

 FREEZER FRIENDLY

Harissa Chicken Thighs with Olives and Potatoes
Serves 4-6

2 tsp harissa spice seasoning (such as the Dunnes Stores Simply Better brand)

2 tsp dried rosemary

1 tsp dried sage

8 skin-on, bone-in chicken thighs

1 tbsp rapeseed oil

1 large onion, thinly sliced

6 carrots, thinly sliced

2 garlic cloves, crushed

2 tbsp tomato purée

600ml (1 pint) chicken stock (from a cube is fine)

500g (1lb 2oz) baby new potatoes, cut into halves or quarters (depending on size)

1 × 100g (4oz) carton or jar of pitted green olives

sea salt and freshly ground black pepper

TO GARNISH

chopped fresh flat-leaf parsley (optional)

Harissa spice seasoning is a dry spice that is now available under the Dunnes Stores Simply Better brand. It imparts a depth of smoky chilli flavour that is incredibly versatile. I find myself reaching for it again and again, as it jazzes up a few simple ingredients into something special.

Preheat your slow cooker according to the manufacturer's instructions.

Mix the harissa spice seasoning with the rosemary and sage in a shallow dish and season lightly with salt and plenty of pepper (the olives will add a natural saltiness to the dish). Use to lightly coat the chicken thighs evenly, shaking off any excess and reusing as necessary.

If your slow cooker has a sauté option, you can use this; if not, use a large sauté pan on the hob over a medium heat. Heat the oil, then add the seasoned chicken thighs, presentation side down. Cook for a couple of minutes, then turn over with a tongs and cook for another minute, until sealed and lightly golden. Transfer to a plate.

Add the onion and carrots to the slow cooker along with the garlic and tomato purée. Pour in the stock, scraping the bottom to remove any browned bits. Stir in the potatoes and olives, then using a tongs, put the chicken on top. Cover and cook on low for 5 hours, until the chicken and potatoes are completely tender.

Arrange the harissa chicken thighs with olives and potatoes in warmed shallow bowls and scatter the parsley on top (if using) to serve.

30 MINS

 4¼ HRS

 LOADS OF VEG

Mushroom and Celeriac Rice Bowl with Parmesan
Serves 4–6

50g (2oz) dried porcini mushrooms

100ml (3½fl oz) boiling water

2 tbsp rapeseed oil

1 onion, finely chopped

2 garlic cloves, finely chopped

300g (11oz) chestnut mushrooms, sliced

400g (14oz) Italian short grain brown rice

1 heaped tbsp fresh thyme leaves, plus extra to garnish

1 small celeriac, peeled and finely diced

1.2 litres (2 pints) vegetable stock (from a cube is fine)

50g (2oz) freshly grated Parmesan cheese

15g (½oz) fresh flat-leaf parsley, leaves stripped and roughly chopped

sea salt and freshly ground black pepper

This is similar to a risotto but uses Italian short grain brown rice, which is the same as white except that the germ of the grain is still attached, making it much more nutritious and higher in fibre. It has a stronger, nuttier taste that stands up well to punchier flavours.

Preheat your slow cooker according to the manufacturer's instructions. Pour the boiling water over the porcini mushrooms and set aside to soak for 10 minutes.

If your slow cooker has a sauté option, you can use this; if not, use a sauté pan on the hob over a medium-high heat. Heat the oil, then add the onion and garlic and sauté for 3–4 minutes, until softened. Stir in the chestnut mushrooms, season with salt and pepper and sauté for another 2–3 minutes, until they soften and release their juices. Stir in the rice and thyme until evenly combined. Place in the slow cooker (if you have used a separate pan).

Drain the porcini mushrooms, reserving the liquid, and finely chop. Add the chopped mushrooms and their soaking liquid to the slow cooker with the celeriac and stock, then season with salt and pepper. Cover and cook on low for 4 hours, until the rice is tender and all of the liquid has been absorbed.

Fold in most of the Parmesan with the parsley and divide between bowls. Scatter over the rest of the Parmesan and a fine sprinkling of fresh thyme leaves to serve.

30 MINS

 6¼ HRS

 LOADS OF VEG

 FREEZER FRIENDLY (BEEF)

Beef and Celeriac with Chestnut Mushrooms and Soured Cream
Serves 4-6

25g (1oz) plain flour

1 tsp sweet paprika, plus a little extra to garnish

500g (1lb 2oz) stewing beef, cut into chunks

2 tbsp rapeseed oil

1 garlic clove, crushed

2 tsp tomato purée

knob of butter

2 banana shallots, finely chopped

200g (7oz) chestnut mushrooms, halved

1 tbsp white wine vinegar

4 tbsp white wine

1 small celeriac, peeled and finely diced

450ml (¾ pint) beef stock (from a cube is fine)

225g (8oz) fresh egg tagliatelle

200ml (7fl oz) soured cream, plus extra to garnish

1 tsp Dijon mustard

sea salt and freshly ground black pepper

TO GARNISH

torn fresh flat-leaf parsley (optional)

I love this recipe! It's hearty, rich and unbelievably flavourful. Plus the slow cooker does most of the work, making it a great recipe for busy weeknights. Chunks of beef with shallots, mushrooms and celeriac are simmered all day. Then, just before serving, freshly cooked egg tagliatelle, soured cream and Dijon mustard are added.

Preheat your slow cooker according to the manufacturer's instructions.

Sprinkle the flour and paprika over the beef and season with salt and pepper. Toss to coat, shaking off any excess. If your slow cooker has a sauté option, you can use this; if not, use a large sauté pan on the hob over a medium heat. Heat 1 tablespoon of the oil, then working in batches, add the beef and quickly sear until golden brown on all sides, turning regularly with a tongs. Transfer to a plate while you continue to cook the remainder. Add the garlic and tomato purée to the last batch of beef, stirring to coat, then transfer to a plate until needed.

Once you've cooked all the beef, add the remaining tablespoon of oil with the butter, then add the shallots and mushrooms and sauté for a couple of minutes. Pour in the vinegar and allow it to bubble right down, then add the wine, scraping the bottom of the pan with a wooden spoon to remove any browned bits. Stir in the celeriac and stock. Place in the slow cooker (if you have used a separate pan), then add the seared beef and any meat juices and season to taste. Cover and cook on low for 6 hours.

When ready to serve, cook the tagliatelle for 2–3 minutes or according to the packet instructions. Stir into the slow cooker with the soured cream and mustard. Leave to rest for 5 minutes to allow the flavours to combine.

Divide between bowls and add a dollop of soured cream, then sprinkle with a little paprika and some parsley (if using) to serve.

20 MINS + SOAKING OVERNIGHT

 10½ HRS

 LOADS OF VEG

Butter Beans with Eggs, Garlicky Yoghurt and Chilli Butter Serves 4–6

225g (8oz) dried butter beans

3 tbsp rapeseed oil

2 onions, finely chopped

1 garlic bulb, finely chopped

1 tsp chopped fresh oregano

good pinch of dried chilli flakes

2 × 400g (14oz) tins of Italian chopped tomatoes

200ml (7fl oz) vegetable stock (from a cube is fine)

1 tbsp sherry or red wine vinegar

pinch of caster sugar

4–6 eggs

200g (7oz) thick Greek yoghurt

sea salt and freshly ground black pepper

FOR THE CHILLI BUTTER

50g (2oz) butter

½ tsp hot chilli powder

squeeze of lemon juice

TO SERVE

chargrilled slices of sourdough bread

This is a version of the Greek fasolia gigantes, which translates as tomato-braised butter beans. If you switch the slow cooker to the 'keep warm' setting, any whole egg yolks will stay runny for up to an hour.

Soak the beans in plenty of cold water overnight, then drain.

Preheat your slow cooker according to the manufacturer's instructions. If your slow cooker has a sauté option, you can use this; if not, use a large sauté pan on the hob over a medium-high heat. Heat the oil, then add the onions and sauté for about 10 minutes, until soft and slightly golden. Stir in all the garlic expect for two cloves (which you'll need for the garlicky yoghurt) along with the oregano and chilli flakes and cook for another minute.

Place in the slow cooker (if you have used a separate pan) and add the beans, tomatoes, stock, vinegar and sugar. Season to taste with salt and pepper, then cover and cook on low for 10 hours, until the beans are meltingly tender.

Turn the heat up to high. Break the eggs on top of the butter bean stew and cook until the eggs are cooked to your liking – 8–12 minutes should do it.

Meanwhile, mix the reserved garlic into the yoghurt in a small bowl and season well.

Heat a small frying pan over a high heat. Add the butter and chilli powder and cook until the butter starts to brown slightly and turn nutty. Add the lemon juice – be careful, as it may splutter a little.

Spoon the beans on the chargrilled sourdough bread, then top with the poached eggs and some garlicky yoghurt. Drizzle over the hot chilli butter and some freshly ground black pepper to serve.

30 MINS + SOAKING OVERNIGHT

 7½ HRS

 LOADS OF VEG

 FREEZER FRIENDLY

225g (8oz) dried haricot beans

250g (9oz) stewing beef, cut into chunks

25g (1oz) seasoned plain flour

2 tbsp rapeseed oil

2 garlic cloves, crushed

2 tbsp tomato purée

1 large onion, chopped

4 large carrots, chopped

8 spring onion and black pepper pork sausages (or similar)

100ml (3½fl oz) red wine

500ml (18fl oz) stout

2 bay leaves

2 tbsp HP brown sauce

1 × 400g (14oz) tin of Italian whole plum tomatoes

sea salt and freshly ground black pepper

TO GARNISH

roughly chopped fresh flat-leaf parsley

Vera's Beef and Sausage Stew
Serves 4-6

My mum always had so many mouths to feed and she was wonderful at making a delicious dinner with very little expense. This recipe is an excellent example of how to use frugal cuts of beef but still make a dish fit for a king!

Soak the beans in plenty of cold water overnight, then drain.

Preheat your slow cooker according to the manufacturer's instructions. Lightly coat the beef in the seasoned flour. If your slow cooker has a sauté option, you can use this; if not, use a large sauté pan on the hob over a medium heat. Heat 1 tablespoon of the oil, then working in batches, add the beef and quickly sear until golden brown on all sides, turning regularly with a tongs. Transfer to a plate while you continue to cook the remainder. Add the garlic and tomato purée to the last batch of beef, stirring to coat, then transfer to a plate until needed.

Once you've cooked all the beef, add the remaining tablespoon of oil to the pan, then add the onion and carrots and sauté for a couple of minutes. Squeeze the sausages out of their skins and break up into pieces, then add to the pan, stirring to coat. Sauté for another 2–3 minutes, until the sausages are lightly browned.

Pour in the wine, scraping the bottom of the pan with a wooden spoon to remove any browned bits. Place in the slow cooker (if you have used a separate pan).

Stir in the stout and add the bay leaves and brown sauce. Break up the tomatoes with your hands, then add those too. Return the seared beef and any meat juices to the slow cooker, then stir in the haricot beans and season to taste with salt and pepper. Cover and cook on low for 7 hours, until the beef is meltingly tender and the beans are cooked through.

Ladle into warmed shallow bowls and scatter over the parsley to garnish.

Index